Mastering Operations

HSC Business Studies Topic 1

Graham Roll

*This book is dedicated to the late Mike Lembach —
friend, colleague & mentor.*

Five Senses Education Pty Ltd
2/195 Prospect Highway
Seven Hills 2147
New South Wales
Australia

Roll, Graham
Mastering Operations HSC Business Studies Topic 1
ISBN 978-1-74130-980-5

Contents

Rationale

This is a student topic book. Its purpose is to provide a concise, yet comprehensive coverage of the Operations topic in the HSC Course. Students are advised to seek other references and case studies in this topic because it is important to read as widely as possible in order to get the most from your study of the topic.

As far as possible, the material is presented in the same order as the Board of Studies syllabus.

This book includes a syllabus outline with Board of Studies outcomes together with the "learn to" aspects of the topic. Students are reminded that assessment task in Business Studies will always relate to syllabus topics and outcomes.

For case studies, students may find that useful information may be obtained by contacting the various chambers of commerce in addition to government departments and by using the internet which will give you up to date information in this area. Indeed, students who are aiming to maximise their performance in Business Studies should research these web sites and read newspaper articles for the most up to date facts and figures.

Topic 1

OPERATIONS

The focus of this topic is to consider the strategies for effective operations management in large businesses.

Overview of Content and Outcomes

There are **four** major areas to be covered in this topic and they are as follows:
- The role of operations management
- Influences on operations
- Operations processes
- Operations strategies

1.1 The Role of Operations Management

- Strategic role of operations management
  - cost leadership
  - good/service differentiation
- Goods and/or services in different industries
- Interdependence with other key business functions

1.2 Influences on Operations

- Globalisation
  - technology
  - quality expectations
  - cost-based competition
  - government policies
  - legal regulation
  - environmental sustainability
- Corporate social responsibility
  - the difference between legal compliance and ethical responsibility
  - environmental sustainability and social responsibility

1.3 Operations Processes

- Inputs
  - transformed resources (materials, information, customers)
  - transforming resources (human resources, facilities)
- Transformation processes
  - the influence of volume, variety, variation in demand and visibility (customer contact)
  - sequencing and scheduling- Gantt charts, critical path analysis
  - technology, task design and process layout
  - monitoring, control and improvement
- Outputs
  - customer service
  - warranties

1.4 Operations Strategies

- Performance objectives
  - quality
  - speed
  - dependability
  - flexibility
  - customisation
  - cost
- New product or service design and development
- Supply chain management
  - logistics
  - e-commerce
  - global sourcing
- Outsourcing
  - advantages and disadvantages
- Technology
  - leading edge, established
  - Inventory management
  - advantages and disadvantages of holding stock
  - LIFO (last-in-first-out)
  - FIFO (first-in-first-out)
  - JIT (just-in-time)
- Quality management
  - control
  - assurance
  - improvement
- Overcoming resistance to change
  - financial costs
  - purchasing new equipment
  - redundancy payments
  - retraining
  - reorganising plant layout
  - inertia
- Global factors
  - global sourcing
  - economies of scale
  - scanning and learning
  - research and development

Outcomes

Linked to the topic content are the topic outcomes. We will go through each of the topic outcomes so that you will understand the **key requirements.** This is important because unless you understand where you are heading then you will not use your study time effectively.

There are **nine** outcomes being covered in this topic and they are to:
- critically analyse the role of business in Australia and globally
- evaluate management strategies in response to changes in internal and external influences
- discuss the social and ethical responsibilities of management
- analyse business functions and processes in large global businesses
- explain management strategies and their impact on business
- evaluate the effectiveness of management in the performance of business
- plan and conduct investigations into contemporary business practices
- organise and evaluate information for actual and hypothetical business situations
- communicate business information, issues and concepts in appropriate formats.

Also important to the understanding of your syllabus content is the section of the syllabus known as the **"learn to"** components of the topic.

Here you are being asked to **examine contemporary business issues** in order to be able to:
- discuss the balance between cost and quality in operations strategy
- examine the impact of globalisation on operations strategy
- identify the breadth of government policies that affect operations management
- explain why corporate social responsibility is a key concern in operations management.

You will need to investigate aspects of business using hypothetical situations and actual business case studies to:
- describe the features of operations management for business in a tertiary industry
- assess the relationship between operations and the other key business functions in two actual businesses
- explain how operations strategy can help a business sustain its competitive advantage
- recommend possible operations strategies for one hypothetical business.

1.1 The Role of Operations Management

Strategic role of operations management

In the Preliminary course we defined operations as the process of converting raw materials into finished goods. **Operations management** refers to the management of that process. Here we are concerned with the allocation and maintenance of machinery and resources. It addresses productivity, quality, wastage and the introduction of new technologies. It may extend to a wider sphere of production such as assembly, batching, creative design and packaging. It is sometimes also referred to as production management.

Focus Point

Operations management can be described as the allocation and maintenance of machinery and resources

Many processes in baking are still done by hand.

Steel making is an example of a simple process.

Operations management

This process can be either simple or elaborate. **Simple processing** refers to the transformation of raw materials into finished products using a small number of stages. For example, the extraction of iron ore for shipment to a steel mill in Australia or overseas is an example of a simple process.

However, when the iron ore is transformed into steel, sorted, graded and then fabricated into a finished good such as the components in a motor vehicle, this is "**elaborately transformed manufacture**" or ETM.

Strategic management of operations relates to decision making about "long term" management issues. "Long term" may be considered as five years or more. Strategic issues include determining the size and location of manufacturing plants, deciding the structure of service or telecommunications networks, and designing technology and supply chains.

Cost Leadership

Professor Michael Porter of Harvard Business School developed the theory of **cost leadership.** This involves producing goods or services at the lowest cost possible to the business. If it can keep its costs low then it will maximise its profits. It describes a way to establish a **competitive advantage** over its competitors.

Companies that choose a **cost leadership** strategy usually offer relatively standardised products with a level of **differentiation** at the lowest competitive price. In this way customers receive the best deal when this strategy is implemented.

Cost leadership strategies include:
- building efficient production facilities
- establishing tight control over overhead costs
- keeping the cost of sales low
- investing in the state of the art manufacturing technologies
- ensuring they source the cheapest raw materials while maintaining quality
- using the best quality labour
- sourcing the best information about competitors and raw materials
- using time and money efficiently
- differentiating the product.

Taken together a business is able to keep its costs as low as possible. The consumer purchases at the most competitive price and the business is able to maximise profits.

Differentiating goods/services

A business uses a number of different devices to differentiate its goods or services from that of its competitors. For example, supermarket chains and airlines find it very difficult to differentiate their products - Woolworths and Coles are very similar. However with the entry of Aldi into the marketplace in recent years, some level of differentiation has been introduced. Where it is difficult to see points of difference, the differentiation is acheived through advertising, price perception, jingles and logos. In this way, these businesses will make their output stand out from its competitors' output and therefore capture greater market share.

The airline industry has the same difficulty in differentiating themselves to their customers: Jetstar or Virgin may not be much different from each other in terms of service and quality.

The airline industry must use catchy jingles and gimmicky promotions to differentiate themselves from their competitors and gain increased market share. However at the end of the day supermarkets and airlines are much the same regardless of their efforts to differentiate themselves. In both cases those businesses have to employ a range of strategies to differentiate their products. For example Woolworths uses the slogan 'Woolworths the fresh food people' and Coles tries to promote itself by using well known personalities who explain how a meal can be produced for less than $10 using the produce from Coles.

Companies use logos for product differentiation.

Almost every business has competitors. Some businesses can differentiate their goods and services more easily than others. Two important strategies are the use of branding and packaging.

Some businesses find differentiation easier because they try to offer a better quality service, and that service is different from business to business. For example Mona Vale Education Centre (a tutoring business on the Northern Beaches of Sydney) is able to offer a good quality service with individualised tutoring by qualified experts (nearly all of whom are qualified practising teachers). In this case while the businesses are in the same industry offering similar services but the differences are strong as opposed to the Woolworths/ Coles or QANTAS/Jetstar/Virgin scenarios.

 If we look at the manufacturing side of the production process and product differentiation, then we can't go past the examples of the automotive industry. Holden, Ford and Toyota, our three largest car sellers in Australia, need to differentiate their vehicles. Now in theory a motor vehicle is something to get us from point A to point B. However these car companies produce many different models to suit their customers. For example Toyota has the Aurion, Avensis, Camry, Corolla, Hiace, Hilux, Kluger, Landcruiser, Tarago and Yaris. Now, **within** the Yaris range there are a further ten models from 3 door to 4 door with different combinations of engine capacities and colour combinations etc. Not only is Toyota providing choice for its customers but it is also providing a point of product differentiation.

Goods and/or services in different industries

The table below provides a conceptual model for analysing the ways goods and sevices may be differentiated in different industries. The model adopted is not necessarily the "correct" one but is simply a basis for comparison.

	mining	retail	tourism	transport	education	steel
packaging	✗	✓	✓	✓	✗	✗
price	✓	✓	✓	✓	✓	✓
source	✓	✗	✗	✗	✗	✓
timeliness	✗	✓	✗	✓	✗	✗
efficiency	✓	✓	✓	✓	✓	✓
technological impact	✓	growing	✗	✓	✗	✓
labour intensive	✗	✓	✓	✗	✓	✗
effectiveness	✓	?	✗	✓	✓	✓

Interdependence with other key business functions

The key business functions are operations, marketing, finance and human resources. Business must synchronise the different functions to ensure they don't operate in isolation. By functioning interdependently it is possible to minimise waste. Effective operations requires:
- goods to be produced for a purpose (Marketing)
- funds available to meet performance schedules (Finance)
- sufficient staff appropriately skilled and trained (Human Resources).

Without coordination, production would be chaotic and indeed may not function at all. Equally, there is no value in developing a sophisticated advertising and promotional campaign to sell a company's product line if the output of the operations department is not matching the demand created by the sales force. It is the role of of the CEO or General Manager to make sure that the various functions are coordinated, and the business runs smoothly.

REVISION EXERCISES 1.1

1. Define and briefly describe "operations management".

   _____

   _____

   _____

   _____

2. Describe an example of an "operations" process.

   _____

   _____

   _____

   _____

   _____

   _____

3. Describe Professor Michael Porter's concept of "cost leadership".

   _____

   _____

   _____

   _____

   _____

4. List the **nine** cost leadership strategies.

   1 _____

   2 _____

   3 _____

   4 _____

   5 _____

   6 _____

   7 _____

   8 _____

   9 _____

REVISION EXERCISES 1.1   **Page 2**

5. What does a business hope to achieve by "differentiating its goods and services"? Give some examples of companies attempting to differentiate their goods and services from their competitors.

_____

_____

_____

_____

_____

_____

_____

_____

_____

_____

_____

_____

_____

6. In the space below explain how the "operations" function is interdependent with other key business functions.

_____

_____

_____

_____

_____

_____

_____

_____

_____

_____

_____

_____

_____

1.2 Influences on Operations

As we move through the 21st Century business constantly finds that there are many things that influence it in all directions. Business is dynamic i.e. it is constantly changing according to the changing circumstances. If we look at the way we did business ten, twenty or thirty years ago we would find that it has changed incredibly.

Operations are impacted by influences arising from:

- globalisation
- technology
- quality expectations
- cost-based competition
- government policies
- legal regulation and
- environmental sustainability.

Globalisation

Globalisation is the bringing together of all of the world's economies for the purposes of trade and culture. It is the removing of trade barriers, language barriers, and cultural barriers. It leads to the freeing up of the movement of labour from one country to another, the unification of laws and the unification of currency. It also involves financial flows, investment, technology and general economic behaviour in and between nations. No longer are brand products exclusive to one or a few countries. A good proportion of the goods we buy today are available all around the world and are produced all around the world. Globalisation is probably the biggest influence on business operations.

> **Focus Point**
>
> *Globalisation is bringing together all of the world's economies for the purposes of trade and culture.*

Goods are often assembled in one country but made from components that are made in several different countries. In the automobile industry a computer program that runs an electronic component in a car may be made by one company and installed in **all** brands of car.

Globalisation of operations has affected all levels of business: primary, secondary and tertiary. In the last century, there had been a distinct increase in demand for natural resources, such as timber, minerals, materials and food. Developed countries often have high levels of demand for primary and secondary industry products. Urban development amongst other things, has reduced the availability of land used for primary production. Local secondary industry has become increasingly less profitable due to rising labour costs.

Tertiary industries are service industries, including tourism, customer assistance and education. This is one of the areas where developed countries can compete with low wages in other countries because many tertiary industries require employees with certain educational standards and, sometimes, specific skills. Tourism, for example, is an industry that cannot be removed from the source country.

The underdeveloped countries are increasingly used as a source for primary production, and as a location for factories producing secondary product, taking advantage of lower wages costs. Globalisation of operations works because resource-poor countries provide the market and the capital to establish commercial activities in countries that still have natural resources.

Globalisation has enabled corporations to relocate secondary operations to countries where the cost of labour and/or equipment is low. If the place of operation is also close to the market where the products will be sold, then the company benefits again from lower distributions costs.

The downside for the labour market is that often, countries with higher standards of living and higher minimum wages lose secondary industries to other countries. Australia's manufacturing industry, for example, has suffered because labour costs in some other countries are cheaper than the equivalent labour here.

Global distribution of technology also plays a role in reducing the labour market for secondary industries. As the cost drops, even poorer countries can start to adopt technology that replaces the work force, which affects unemployment.

Globalisation, therefore affects all three tiers of operations, but in different ways. Globalisation provides a market for primary industries, but demand can sometimes take priority over sustainability. Secondary industries benefit from globalisation because corporations choose areas where the market suits them, but this may lead to unemployment for skilled workers who live in countries with a higher standard of living. Globalisation, combined with technology, is an advantage for tertiary industries when corporations can sell services on the global marketplace without relocation.

Another aspect of globalisation in the production process has been the concept of vertical integration i.e. an oil company which owns the oil tankers, owns the oil refineries and owns the service stations. As globalisation has proceeded, vertical integration has increased more and more. This concept of vertical integration has come about as a way of ensuring the supply of raw materials for the business if they own all stages of the production process.

Technology

Technology has a great influence on operations

Technology has also had a great influence on operations. Business must access the latest technology in order to compete effectively. In the end new technology will make operations cheaper and more efficient.

Technology may influence some tertiary industries that are not location specific. Call centres in the customer assistance industry, for example, can be relocated to any place that contains employees who speak the language of the source country.

Some of the technologies that have been employed in recent years include
- robotics which helps business with some of the more difficult processes and saves on staff
- automated and computerised assembly lines which speed up the production process and improves accuracy
- computer aided design (CAD) allowing the computer to take over the design process.
- computer aided manufacture (CAM) is software which allows the manufacturing process to become controlled by a computer
- scanning systems and bar coding- particularly used for stock control
- wireless computer systems and modems
- smart phones that enable communication all around the world via internet at the swipe of a finger
- assorted other technologies that have been around for several years now including satellite navigation systems and swipe cards etc.

Quality Expectations

Quality expectations are sometimes known as quality assurance and are procedures within a business designed to improve or maintain all aspects of quality in the production process to make it more efficient. There are a number of recognised quality management approaches used in the production process and these include:

- **inspection of output** at each stage of the production process to ensure that this output reaches the required standards for further processing or sale to the customer. If it is not possible to inspect every item, sampling techniques may be employed. The results of the testing will determine whether the output will be accepted or rejected.

- **world's best practice** is a policy objective adopted by business to ensure the highest standards are applied. **World's best practice** could refer to production, marketing, administration, IT or research and development. Global benchmarks are set by multinational business to ensure an equivalent performance standard in all operations around the world regardless of the location or nationality of the operation. For example, car component manufacturers will apply international quality standards to components manufactured in Australia, China, Malaysia or any other place in the world.
  World's best practice is becoming more and more common in the production process. With most of the world's largest companies sending their production off-shore, the standard of output must be the same as if the product was made in Japan, USA or Australia.

- **Total Quality Management (TQM)** is a concept in business where all employees are involved in programs to achieve the best possible standards of quality throughout all aspects of the business. It was an American idea applied to Japanese manufacturing after the Second World War (1950s) It has now become accepted and adapted world wide.

- **quality Circles** comprise groups of skilled employees gathered together in a process that aims to better the quality of a product/service or procedure that will benefit a customer or the business by decreasing unnecessary costs.

- **Kaizen** is the Japanese concept of constantly seeking improvement and questioning current methods of production. Workers work on achieving higher standards and improving the way they do things.

Cost-based Competition

Cost-based pricing involves working out all your costs, including overheads, adding a profit margin and then setting a pricing policy for a firm's output. With **competition based pricing** on the other hand, the pricing policy is determined by the market. The business will deduct its operating costs , including overheads, from the market price to determine its operating profit. **Cost-based pricing** may be usefully applied where competitive forces are relatively weak, or in periods of high or unsatisfied demand.

Government Policies

Every business has to respect and adhere to government policies with regard to production. There are several reasons for this. Firstly, government needs to ensure safety and quality standards. The safety standards relate to consumer safety. For example seat belts in cars for adults and children must be of a certain standard in order to restrain the occupants in the event of an accident. Manufacturers must comply with these standards or face heavy penalties. Quality is important for the consumer. Goods produced by an Australian manufacturer or goods imported from overseas must reach certain standards of quality.

Government policies often relate to our export industries such as the wine industry. Because Australia receives a great deal of export income from the export of our wines, it is important to ensure that those exports are of the highest quality and that Australia's reputation remains high. The following extract from the Department of Foreign Affairs and Trade website demonstrates this:

"Australia maintains national standards for wine that are administered by state and territory governments. Federal regulations focus on quality control. The Australian federal government assists the industry by improving the trade environment (redressing barriers to trade) and by improving the domestic economic operating environment. Policy issues are the province of the Australian Government Department of Agriculture, Fisheries and Forestry. The Australian Wine and Brandy Corporation promotes and controls the export of wine and brandy.

The Grape and Wine Research and Development Corporation is the body responsible for investing in grape and wine research and development, on behalf of the Australian wine industry and the Australian community. Australia's reputation as one of the most technologically advanced wine-producing nations owes much to the industry's emphasis on research and development. Key research and development sources include the Australian Wine Research Institute, the Commonwealth Scientific and Industrial Research Organisation, the National Wine and Grape Industry Centre, state departments of agriculture and universities.

Australia is one of the most technologically advanced wine producing countries in the world.

Legal Regulation

An important influence on operations is the regulation imposed on business by all levels of government. Regulation is good for consumers as well as business. For example a food product must meet certain health standards for the consumer. Companies need to provide clean and sterile conditions for the production of food products. Health regulations governing food production, distribution, service and consumption are the responsibility of many government authorities: federal, state and local. A good example is the dairy industry which is strictly regulated.

Regulations may affect a business and the welfare of its workers. Where the work is dangerous then management must ensure (by law) that employees are looked after under Occupational Health & Safety legislation.

Naming Rights and the Law

Property rights such as naming rights are regulated and enforced by law.

In the wine industry, there are many sparkling wines produced worldwide, yet most legal structures reserve the term "champagne" exclusively for sparkling wines from the Champagne region of France. In the European Union and many other countries, the name Champagne is legally protected by the Treaty of Madrid (1891) designating only the sparkling wine produced in the eponymous region of France can be called champagne. This legal protection has been accepted by numerous other countries worldwide. Most recently Canada, Australia, and Chile signed agreements with Europe that will limit the use of the term "champagne" to only those products produced in the Champagne region.

In the same way in North America, whiskey sold as Tennessee whiskey is also defined as Bourbon and is required to meet the legal definition of Bourbon. However, under Canadian law some makers of Tennessee whiskey do not label their product as Bourbon and insist that it is a different type of whiskey when marketing their product.

The legal definition of Bourbon may vary somewhat from country to country, although various trade agreements require the name Bourbon to be reserved for products made in the United States. The U.S. regulations for the labelling and advertising of Bourbon apply only to products made for consumption within the United States; they do not apply to distilled spirits made for export. Canadian law requires products labelled as Bourbon to be made in the United States and to also conform to the requirements that apply within the United States. However, in countries other than the United States and Canada, products labelled as Bourbon may not adhere to the same standards. European Union regulations require products labelled as Bourbon to be made in the United States, but do not require them to conform to all of the requirements that apply within the United States.

Environmental Sustainability

Over the past 30 years, we have become increasingly concerned about the effect of business operations on the environment. Business has moved away from simply exploiting the natural resources for profit to a position which includes a duty of care for the environment. Public concern about the action of business damaging the environment has been influential in this change of direction.

Previously, commentators raised concerns about the adequacy of natural resources to sustain raging economic growth. Damage was occurring to the air, in the water and on land. Such groups as The Australian Conservation Foundation and Friends of the Earth have been vocal critics of past business behaviour. Legislation has also been directed towards manufacturers of products to become more environmentally friendly. The idea that products and services may be regarded as environmentally friendly has become a feature of today's advertising and marketing programs. The need to reduce the amount of packaging going to landfill has led to many firms producing environmentally friendly packaging. This has been very evident in the take-away food industry.

Current concerns for the projected impact of climate change has had an impact on business policy. Governments have promoted changes in the tax system, including carbon tax to be collected from businesses emitting carbon dioxide. These changes in tax policy, if implemented, will cause changes in business operations.

Social pressure has been significant in changing laws and regulations as political pressure is exerted upon governments to change policy towards operations. The Environment Protection Authority is a government body charged with the responsibility of policing the emissions and waste disposal actions of business.

Consumers are demanding ecologically sound raw materials, packaging, transport and disposal methods.

Corporate social responsibility

Corporate social responsibility is the obligation that business has to other businesses, individuals and organisations. Every business is a part of a wider community: business must perform ethically, respecting the goals and aspirations of others in that community.

The difference between legal compliance and ethical responsibility

Legal compliance derives from the imposition of rules and regulations from an external source. Ethical responsibility derives from the application of moral standards from within the organisation. These ideas are often influences by ideas prevailing in society. Often there is no difference between ethical corporate behaviour, and the practices enforced by legal sanction. Ethical businesses will choose to act responsibly regardless of whether it is legally required to do so.

Environmental sustainability and social responsibility

Socially responsible behaviour is driven by society itself. Over time, the attitudes of society change. For example in the 1950s and 1960s, it was quite acceptable to dump waste anywhere. Since the 1970s the attitudes of society have changed and pressure groups such as Greenpeace have put pressure on governments to change laws in favour of the environment. In the 21st century environmental laws have been enhanced and indeed most businesses see their environmental responsibility as a normal part of their goals and aspirations.

REVISION EXERCISES 1.2

1. Define globalisation.

_____

_____

_____

_____

_____

2. Outline how the production process is affected by globalisation.

_____

_____

_____

_____

_____

_____

3. Explain the effects of technology on the production process and list **eight** examples of technology used in the production process.

1 _____

2 _____

3 _____

4 _____

5 _____

6 _____

7 _____

8 _____

4. What is another name for "quality expectations" and what does it refer to? Give **five** examples of these "quality expectations".

1 _____

2 _____

3 _____

4 _____

5 _____

REVISION EXERCISES 1.2 Page 2

5. Describe "cost based competition".

   _____

   _____

6. Outline **two** ways in which "government policies" have had an influence on production. Why is government interested in business production?

   _____

   _____

7. Give **four** examples of "legal regulations" that can affect production.

   _____

   _____

   _____

   _____

   _____

8. Outline why "environmental sustainability" is important to the production process.

   _____

   _____

   _____

   _____

9. Define "corporate social responsibility".

   _____

   _____

10. Outline the differences between "legal compliance and ethical responsibility" and "environmental sustainability and social responsibility".

    _____

    _____

    _____

    _____

    _____

1.3 Operations Processes

Business operations involves a number of complementary and often sequential processes. These processes consist of inputs, transformation processes and outputs, arranged as follows:

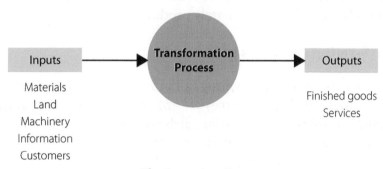

The Operations Process

Inputs

Transformed resources

Inputs are the resources used in operations. Three inputs we need to consider here are:
- materials
- information and
- customers.

Materials

These are the raw materials used in operations. The bakery that we considered earlier will use flour, water, salt and yeast to make the bread. It may use a variety of other ingredients if it is baking other types of bread. These materials are then transformed to make the finished product. **A service business** such as tutoring will use stationery, computers and text books etc.

Information

This is used in a business in order to help transform the raw materials into finished products. Information in the form of new research from a University may help a business to produce their product in a more efficient, cost effective manner. **Market research** information may help the business to target their customers more precisely. This information could be about the demographic characteristics (income, age structure, ethnicity, sex, education etc) of the market and this may involve primary and secondary research designed to discover the buying patterns and habits of these customers. This information is then used (transformed) to help the business with its production decisions.

Customers

Customers are part of the inputs and the outputs. They ideally will have some influence over what is produced and as consumers they represent the main target for what is ultimately produced.

Transforming resources

Resources used for transforming fall into two categories: Human resources and Facilities. Human resources are enhanced by a number of influences, primarily training and education, although demographic, cultural and socioeconomic factors all play their part.

Human resources:
- Factory staff are individuals within the factory who produce the product.
- Designers are involved across product design, visual representation and informational elements concerned with the product. They are also engaged in packaging and the presentation to market.
- Marketers are concerned with the communication and delivery of value to customers. They also have the responsibility to manage customer relationships which will in turn benefit the organisation and its stakeholders.
- Accountants are in charge of the administration of financial aspects of the business.
- Sales Staff are responsible for the day to day communications with customers.

Facilities:
- Manufacturing Plant
- Storage
- Logistics

Up-to-date facilities and the latest technology have a significant impact on how operations are performed. A manufacturing plant will be more efficient, if everything works properly and if out-of-date procedures are eliminated.

Transformation processes

Converting inputs into outputs involves complex processes. The transformation process is influenced by a number of factors: volume, variety, variation in demand and visibility.

Volume

When goods are produced in greater volumes there are a number of effects.
- economies of scale allow goods to be produced more cheaply.
- greater volumes ensure that upward variations in demand can be easily met.
- more effective quality control can be applied to production processes, reducing difficulties when goods are sold.

Variety

Operations meeting consumer demands with a variety of models or alternatives are able to more completely satisfy individual differences expressed by customers. Henry Ford, launching the model T, told his customers that his new car would only be supplied in 1 colour: black. Today's motor vehicle industry supplies a myriad of models with every possible option. Product variation is the key to complete customer satisfaction.

Variation in demand

This term is used to describe how businesses contact their customers. Variation in demand needs to be involved within the transformation process. These variations could be the result of several factors, or trends in demand concerned by economic or market conditions. For certain classes of activities technology and fashion would influence varieties in demand.

Visibility

This refers to the way businesses interact with their customers. Visibility is an important and emerging issue in the retail industry in Australia. Customers contact their suppliers in a number of ways. For retailers, this involves many outlets with extensive stock displays, sophisticated marketing programs; all in the context of competitive pricing. With more and more goods being purchased online, traditional suppliers such as Harvey Norman, David Jones and Myer are facing reduced demand. This can be directly attributed to a reduction in customer contact with these retailers. Physical customer contact isn't necessarily a prerequisite to increased sales. Online retailers have an advantage once they are visible. Current taxation laws allow internet sales to be GST free. Lower overheads allow these sellers to operate using slimmer margins.

Visibility Case Study

Harvey Norman considers customer contact now and in the future.

Gerry Harvey and his wife, Harvey Norman's operating boss Katie Page are very shrewd. They have been proven to be shrewd investors, retailers and landlords. The fact that Harvey Norman initially did not sell online had more to do with a perception of not needing to as well as the perception that online would force their retail prices down. They needed to be seen to protect their franchisees. It was by no means a simple decision to start selling online and there are compelling reasons to do so.

Harvey Norman franchisees are now well served by an e-commerce platform that informs customers before they walk into their store where things are. Whilst online shoppers do compare prices, they are savvy and base their purchase decisions on more than just price. With this in mind, Harvey Norman maintains a broad appeal selling online (as well as winning new customers) because the same things that appeal to their customers offline such as customer service, product warranties, finance options etc, appeal online.

Far from being a "waste of time", Harvey Norman is likely to invest more in e-commerce in coming years because it reflects what customers want and how they are already shopping – almost 58% of Christmas shoppers say they use the internet to research and compare products, according to recent research from the Australian Retailers Association.

However, digital marketing channels are important. It is because times are tough that Harvey Norman needs to consider embracing these digital marketing channels on TV, which are very measurable, will provide new customer information, generate some incremental sales and, perhaps most importantly for the large traditional retailers, increase the likelihood that customers going into a store will buy a product. As more and more international and local suppliers sell direct to the consumer and large retail competitors start to reap the rewards of the online trading the more likely that Harvey Norman will increase online trading.

At a recent Shop.org conference in Las Vegas for the leading US online retailers, Toby Lenk, CEO of Gap.com said that the chief value of their e-commerce effort was to provide a marketing program for stores and that in getting that right, the e-commerce operations themselves had become considerably profitable. He pointed out that online retail was growing at a Compound Annual Growth Rate (CAGR) of 14% compared to a CAGR in traditional retail of 2%. Furthermore, the economics of online trading far outweigh those of offline, with a much higher Return on Invested Capital and lower overall costs.

The Harvey Norman team are known to hold US retailer Best Buy in high regard. Best Buy generates 13% of its USD $1.78bn revenue online and this fact won't have escaped the Aussie retailer (who incidentally would generate more than $300m online if they could replicate this in Australia). Their site has over 14m unique visitors a month and converts them into sales at an average rate of 2%, with an average order size of $210. Granted, Australia is not the US and we have some genuine structural issues (like the size and geographic spread of the population) that make e-commerce tougher here. Nonetheless the size of the prize is growing and Australian retailers have enough information to get this right.

Harvey Norman must also be aware of their competitors' activity. Of their major competitors, most are becoming increasingly active in the online space. Myer is selling online now, with plans to expand to a larger e-commerce operation in future years. Woolworths is investing in online commerce through Dick Smith Electronics, Big W, Tandy and its online supermarket business. Wesfarmers is evaluating how to bring Target and Kmart into a truly multi-channel businesses and expand the Coles online offering. Also JB Hi-Fi has launched its Digital Home electronics site in addition to its existing site for music, DVDs and games. These players are being driven by the desire to stay relevant to their customers and provide a more thorough multi-channel opportunity to buy products because they know it produces better buyer knowledge and that the customer that walks into a store having already been online to research is a more valuable one. Competition is coming from other quarters too, with international retailers starting to take an interest in the Australian retail scene

Management at Harvey Norman and their franchisees are asking themselves whether the growth in online retail demonstrates genuine retail growth, or whether it comes at the expense of traditional sales. It is likely that on-line marketing will pay dividends. This is supported by the experiences of retailers like Gap and Best Buy and now universally acknowledged amongst the world's leading retailers.

There are thousands of online retailers in Australia making good profits. With many of these businesses investing heavily for growth in the area because they can see the changes in the way Australians want to shop and they see the opportunity to establish themselves using international best practice.

Sourced from www.digitalministry.com

Mastering Operations HSC Business Studies Topic 1

Sequencing and scheduling

In order to output a product (especially in a large business) a large amount of organisation needs to go into the process. Sequencing and scheduling are two tools that are used to achieve this goal. Sequencing involves placing tasks into an order so that the whole operation runs smoothly. For example if a building company is constructing a house, there is a certain sequence of events that must take place. You can't put the roof on before the frame is in place, there is no point trying to wire the house after the walls have been installed. Likewise you would not deliver the copper piping for the plumbing before construction starts.

Scheduling involves the time taken to complete a particular job. In our house building exercise above, the site may need three days to complete, two days to dig the footings and one day to lay the foundations. A week may go by for the foundations to harden and then a week may be allowed to lay the brick work etc. This is a schedule.

The same thing occurs in a factory setting. A sequence of events needs to be planned out so that resources are not left idle while the rest of the sequence is taking place and a schedule needs to be devised so that the assembly process runs smoothly.

Gantt Charts may be used for sequencing and Critical Path Analysis will help with scheduling.

Gantt Charts

A Gantt chart is sequencing tool presented as a bar graph with time and activities shown on the two axes as the following examples show. The manager knows how long a particular task should take and whether they are 'on schedule' or not. It also shows which tasks can be done simultaneously or at least overlapping.

Critical Path Analysis and PERT are powerful tools that help a business to schedule and manage complex projects. As with *Gantt Charts*, Critical Path Analysis (CPA) or the Critical Path Method (CPM) helps the business to plan all tasks that must be completed as part of a project. They act as the basis both for preparation of a schedule, and of resource planning. During management of a project, they allow the business to monitor achievement of project goals. They help the manager to see where remedial action needs to be taken to get a project back on course.

Gantt Chart

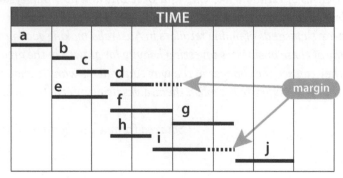

Gantt Chart: Reverse Engineering Project

Tasks	February		March			April			May
	19	22	3	8	12	9	23	30	7
Assign Teams	███								
Select Reverse Engr. Project		███							
Write Proposal		███							
Make Charts & Diagrams			███						
Mechanical Dissection			███						
Competant Sketching					██				
Computer Modelling					███				
Materials Analysis						███			
Writing Final Report		███████████████████							

Critical Path Analysis

Within a project it is likely that a business will display its final project plan as a Gantt Chart. The benefit of using CPA within the planning process is to help them develop and test plans to ensure that they are going to work. Critical Path Analysis identifies tasks which must be completed on time for the whole project to be completed on time. It also identifies which tasks can be delayed if resource needs to be reallocated to catch up on missed or overrunning tasks. A further benefit of Critical Path Analysis is that it helps the business manager to identify the minimum length of time needed to complete a project.

As with Gantt Charts, the essential concept behind Critical Path Analysis is that you cannot start some activities until others are finished. These activities need to be completed in a sequence, with each stage being more-or-less completed before the next stage can begin. These are 'sequential' activities.

Occasionally some activities are not dependent on completion of any other tasks. These may be non-dependent or 'parallel' tasks are not on the critical path and may be completed at any time.

Critical Path Analysis

Pert Sequence Diagram

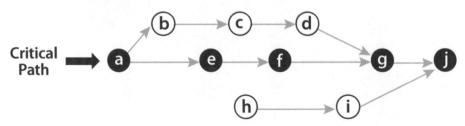

Technology

If a business employs the latest technology, it is likely that it will operate more efficiently than an older plant. Computerisation has been instrumental in bringing operations processes to a higher level. A forward looking business will invest in research and development to ensure technology helps them to continue in this path. The impact of technology will be further explored in section 1.4.

Computer Control Room

Task Design

This involves breaking down complex operations into a series of simple and easy tasks. The project manager will design the procedures to enable the operators (factory workers) to complete the tasks quickly and easily. Any student who has done woodwork or textiles would have had similar experiences. An assignment to design and produce a major work, will involve analysis of the tasks to determine the best way to complete the project. A guiding principle in task design is to ensure that each step in the process is able to be completed by the relevant operator.

The design process also involves the allocation of human resources so that the most appropriate staff are appointed according to their skills and experience. This process saves the business money because the job is completed in minimum time, with maximum efficiency.

Proper Task Design ensures skilled staff are assigned to complex tasks.

Process Layout

Process layout involves the physical layout of the factory or office. If the assembly line or office is poorly designed then the transformation process will be inefficient. OH & S must also be considered in establishing proper layouts.

Features of good layout design:

- **Flexibility.** The firm has the ability to handle a variety of processing requirements.
- **Cost.** Sometimes, the general-purpose equipment utilised may be less costly to purchase and less costly and easier to maintain than specialised equipment.
- **Motivation.** Employees in this type of layout will probably be able to perform a variety of tasks on multiple machines, as opposed to the boredom of performing a repetitive task on an assembly line. A process layout also allows the employer to use some type of individual incentive system.
- **System protection.** Since there are multiple machines available, process layouts are not particularly vulnerable to equipment failures.

A physical layout of a factory is important in the production process.

Process layouts in factories

Process layouts are found primarily in job shops, or firms that produce customised, low-volume products that may require different processing requirements and sequences of operations. Process layouts are configurations in which operations of a similar nature or function are grouped together. As such, they occasionally are referred to as functional layouts.

A manufacturing example would be a machine shop. A machine shop generally has separate departments where general-purpose machines are grouped together by function (e.g., milling, grinding, drilling, hydraulic presses, and lathes). Therefore, facilities that are configured according to individual functions or processes have a process layout. This type of layout gives the firm the flexibility needed to handle a variety of routes and process requirements. Services that utilise process layouts include hospitals, banks, auto repair, libraries, and universities.

www.enotes.com/management-encyclopedia/layout

Monitoring, control and improvement

Monitoring, controlling and improving is a continuous activity. Gantt charts and critical path analysis are useful devices available to managers for observing and managing transformation processes. Improvement on the other hand may require lateral or creative thinking. Effective managers will be aware (monitoring), they will exercise supervision producing action(control), and will take whatever steps required to replan and redirect to pursue the goals of the business (improvement).

- **Inventory control:** Inventory control has a critical impact on the productivity and profitability of a business. Having too much stock may mean that the working capital of a business is curtailed: too much money is tied up in stock and there will be additional expense involved in the management of that stock. Under ordering may lead to delays in the production process until extra stock arrives. Poor inventory control increases the risk of theft by staff or customers. Regular stocktakes i.e. counting of stock on hand will help with stock management by knowing how much is being used/sold in a given period of time and how much needs to be ordered.
- **Production Management:** Manufacturing businesses will usually have a specialist production manager responsible for the efficient operation of the production process. The manger's task will range from the economical use of inputs, the efficient operation of transformation processes, and the effective provision of outputs (products!). To help in this process the manager may use all or some of:
  - Quality management to ensure that internal quality standards are being maintained at every level within the business. This will involve monitoring (testing) inputs, processes and outputs at different points of the production process.
  - Total Quality Management (TQM).
  - Kaizen (continuous improvement).
  - Quality Circles where staff work together to solve problems within the firm.
- **Records management.** Without proper records management a business cannot function efficiently. Records such as data bases, accounting records, inventory records, correspondence all have to be kept in an easy to find and reliable situation. In addition to this, there are legal requirements to be met. The ATO and OSR (Office of State Revenue) and ASIC all require businesses to keep accurate records to reflect the data included in mandatory reports required by these organisations. Personnel and payroll records must be accurately maintained because the business has a duty of care towards its staff. Good records management will enable a manager to take advantage of opportunities as they arise.

Stock management is important in business operations.

Outputs

Outputs are the end result of the operations process. For manufacturing operations, outputs are represented by finished goods. For service operations, outputs are not as visible. For example the school system delivers educational outcomes for students, students pass exams and leave to pursue a career path. Here it is possible to experience the results produced by the output, without seeing the output itself.

Factors useful in assessing outputs are:
- the quality of customer service on delivery
- the guarantees or warranties provided by the business
- the after sales service delivered by the business.

Customer service

Maximising customer service is one of the most important functions of management. Any business that doesn't try to maximise the service it delivers to its customers is leaving itself open to attack from its competition.

A satisfied customer will act as an ambassador for the business. A dissatisfied customer, in telling others about the experience, will have a negative influence on the sales and marketing efforts of the business.

Actions which maximise customer service in the minds of consumers include
- satisfaction with the quality of the product
- satisfaction with the way in which sales staff interact with the customer
- satisfaction with the after sales service.

A business may use a number of devices to monitor the effectiveness of its customer service performance. These include:
- Mystery shopper programs. An actor may visit a retail store and pretend to be a customer. Management receives a report on how the sales staff dealt with the mystery shopper.
- Consumer Research Surveys. Customers are asked questions about their experiences dealing with customer service staff. Customer service policy improvements may arise from these reports.

Warranties

Focus Point

A warranty is an agreement and a period of time when a manufacturer must repair or replace a product that has broken down after purchase.

All products have a warranty. A warranty is an agreement and a period of time when a manufacturer must repair or replace a product that has broken down after purchase. Even a small inexpensive item has an implied warranty that it will do the job it is designed to do. Expensive items such as cars and new houses will have a written warranty. If the product doesn't do what it is supposed to, the customer is entitled to inform the manufacturer and have the problem fixed. In the case of a small, inexpensive items the customer is entitled to a refund or exchange.

As opposed to a condition, a breach of a warranty doesn't entitle the customer to cancel the contract, but they are entitled to sue for damages for non-compliance with warranty conditions. For example, the purchaser of a faulty motor vehicle can sue the car company if it refuses to fix items on the car that are covered by the warranty.

Statutory Warranties

When purchasing goods, regardless of the written warranty given, there are usually implied conditions determined by the nature of the purchase. A refrigerator may have a 12 months warranty, but a purchaser may reasonably expect the appliance to give reliable service for longer. By invoking these implied conditions, a consumer may reasonably expect the supplier to fix the appliance if it breaks down after 12 months. A five star hotel would be expected to provide luxury service to justify the tariff charged, and would be liable to provide compensation if the service was sub-standard.
Implied conditions may include:

- right to sell the goods, the goods are unencumbered and the consumer has the right to quiet enjoyment
- goods will comply with their description
- goods will be of merchantable quality and fit for the purpose
- goods will comply with a sample
- services will be rendered with due care and skill and goods supplied with the service will be fit for purpose; services will be fit for the purpose.

After Sales Service

A large business often utilises the assets of many stakeholders. In a competitive world customers will choose products and services from those offered from different sources. Repeat business will often depend on how well the business met the customer's needs, and how well the business addressed the customers demands after the service or goods had been delivered. This service after sales is now regarded as an essential part of the output from an operations process. A good example is the car industry where service and reliability form part of the product mix and marketing programs for new vehicle sales.

REVISION EXERCISES 1.3

1. From the mini-case study on Harvey Norman on page 28, outline Harvey Norman's proposed future customer contact and online selling policy.

    _____

    _____

    _____

    _____

    _____

2. Outline what "sequencing" and "scheduling" are.

    _____

    _____

    _____

    _____

3. What is a Gantt chart and explain how it is used in production?

    _____

    _____

    _____

4. Define and explain the process involved in the use of a PERT diagram.

    _____

    _____

    _____

    _____

    _____

    _____

5. Explain using an example, the term "process layout".

    _____

    _____

    _____

    _____

    _____

6. Outline **four** advantages of "process layouts."

    1. _____

    2. _____

    3. _____

    4. _____

7. The production process needs to be monitored and controlled. Describe the concepts of:

    – Inventory control

    _____

    _____

    _____

    – Management control

    _____

    _____

    _____

    – Records management

    _____

    _____

    _____

8. Outputs need to be measured in terms of "customer service" and "warranties". Explain the two concepts and outline the advantages of monitoring them.

    _____

    _____

    _____

    _____

9. What is an implied condition?

    _____

    _____

    _____

1.4 Operations Strategies

Operations strategies used to achieve output objectives will be different for each business. These strategies will derive from the corporate plan and objectives of the business. The focus of the strategies may relate to performance, social and cultural factors, or even simply the aspirations of the business owners and stakeholders.

Performance objectives

Quality control is the basis of efficient and effective performance. Management procedures that are put in place to check the suitability of raw materials going into the transformation process, the monitoring of work in progress and output, all contribute to smooth operations. It also helps avoid producing seconds, wastage, increased costs, warranty claims and service problems. Performance objectives include

- quality
- speed
- dependability
- flexibility
- customisation and
- cost.

Quality

This can be described as the level of excellence of a good or service. Most businesses try to produce a quality output whether it be a good or service. In that way they will maximise their profits. When we say quality we mean quality for the price. Obviously we cannot compare the quality of a top of the range Mercedes Benz motor car with that of a Hyundai Getz but there is at least a $100,000 difference in price. However the Hyundai is very good value for money.

As stated above in section 1.2 there are ways of ensuring that quality is produced and these are:

- inspection of output at each stage of the production process
- ensuring world's best practice
- implementing Total Quality Management (TQM)
- implementing Quality Circles
- implementing Kaizen which is the Japanese concept of constantly seeking improvement.

Speed

It is important for a business to produce its output quickly. When an order is received it must be produced and shipped in the time stated to the customer.

If this is not done the reputation of the business is at stake. Customers don't want to hear your hard luck story. While they may be sympathetic, delivery is what they want. However while it is important to produce output on time, speed should not create a problem with quality of output.

Dependability

This is another important operations strategy. Customers want dependability when dealing with a business. Dependability might refer to a representative or trades person turning up on time to give a quote. That quote might need to be emailed, faxed or posted to the customer. This should be done promptly and at the specified time.

When the customer accepts the job, they should be kept informed about the progress of their order and when the starting date will be. Once this is determined there should be no changing of that date except in exceptional circumstances. Even on the starting date, the trades people should turn up on time to start work. If the above seems obvious, one only has to listen to the stories that people talk about regarding unreliable trades people.

In cases when it is business to business such as a retail firm waiting for a delivery of goods for sale to the public, it is important that the goods be delivered on time because it could cost the retailer sales. Sometimes it might be intermediate goods which forms part of the raw materials to make a finished product, that a manufacturer is relying on. If these inputs are late in arriving then the whole production process could be held up, costing the business money. Dependability of supply is essential if a business is to maintain its reputation.

.Whether the finished product such as a refrigerator delivered to a retail customer or an intermediate good delivered to a manufacturer to be used as a component part in a further stage of production, that product should not be faulty. The customer must be able to feel that the product they have purchased is dependable.

Dependable delivery is another important operations strategy.

Flexibility

Inflexible marketing and sales policies may in some circumstances be bad for business. For example if a customer needs to change an order at a late stage then the business must be able to accommodate that change providing the request for a change is not unreasonable. Flexibility may also apply to payment terms for services, or staff employment hours. Technology has allowed management to relax previously inflexible operating conditions to take account of the individual needs of different stakeholders. A business that is not flexible runs the risk of not being adaptable to change. In recent years, the need to be flexible has required some businesses to change structurally. Some of the structural responses to change that are important here are outsourcing, flat structures, networks and strategic alliances.

Outsourcing

Increasingly business contracts certain work "out" to professionals such as lawyers and accountants. Initially this was done for financial reasons: smaller businesses could not afford to employ any of these professionals fulltime. Recently there has been a trend for businesses of all sizes to outsource much of their work to access the best talent available. For example there are many companies contracting out their manufacturing processes. This is further explored on page 51.

Flat Structures

As a response to change, flatter management structures have become more common over the past ten years. Businesses adopt a flatter management structure to reduce the number of levels of management, giving greater responsibility to middle managers.

The traditional hierarchical business structure with many layers of management is not efficient when rapid communication is necessary and when there are several autonomous business units working within the business. In this respect the business is able to more quickly adapt to change, rather than having several layers of management to work through in order to implement change.

Networks

Network theory relates to the connections between social entities (individuals, groups, organisations,etc) because they come into contact with each other. Within a business some of these connections are formalised when people are placed in work groups, or if they are required to communicate with each other according to a formal organisation structure. In practice, the degree of interaction and communication is much more extensive because we all belong to a multiplicity of groups or networks.

The common bond may be for social or cultural reasons, it may exist because we share common interests, or we might live in the same community. Networks could be accidental, or they may exist because we intend to join a group. Participating in a network is called"networking".

A business-based network might be an industry group such as The Society of Accountants, The Institution of Engineers, or The Chamber of Commerce. The sales managers and salesmen involved in the stationary supply industry regularly play golf on a pre=arranged date to enjoy themselves socially, but also to engage in "networking". In all these cases individuals of similar backgrounds will meet regularly to discuss items of common interest at their network meetings.

Strategic Alliances

A strategic alliance is a network established for a particular purpose. It usually will be based on a formal agreement binding each participant to pursue a common goal. They are usually established when each partner is able to contribute to the alliance in a unique way. One partner to the alliance may be unable to fulfil the requirements alone, but may be empowered to proceed utilising the complementary skills provided by the other party.

Examples of strategic alliances in business include:
- a manufacturing business possessing advantages in production might enter into an agreement with a distribution company to better access its customers at a lower cost.
- a business wanting to expand overseas could form an alliance with a business in the target country to avoid establishing a new office in an overseas country, often avoiding expensive start-up costs. The overseas business benefits from increased growth and activity.

Strategic alliances provide speed and flexibility to each business partner. They are able to access the resources of the other party immediately, without incurring the expense of setting up their own capability. Technology is often the trigger for strategic alliances. A business may be unable to afford a new production machine which revolutionises its traditional activity. It may solve this problem by joining with similar businesses to buy the machine, sharing the cost, and taking turns in utilising its output for their respective customers. Recently a number of "offset" printers in Sydney set up a "digital printing" hub, owned by each one jointly to do just this.

Customisation

Customisation refers to the creation and supply of a product according to a customer's individual requirements. Individual requirements may be satisfied by offering alternatives as options. In reality most products don't need to be customised; Consumer goods can be taken from the shelf and customised. In choosing a television, the only point of difference might be the size or appearance. Most televisions today come equipped with the capacity support a range of standard applications. Customisation is achieved by providing a choice of options
Kitchen manufacturers will **customise** a kitchen based on the client's brief, budget and design constraints determined by the construction site.

Cost

Cost minimisation is a significant performance objective. Profitability, cost and quality all affect each other. A business that cuts corners to keep costs down will find that quality will suffer. Declining quality will reduce sales and therefore profits. The interdependent nature of operations strategies requires a business manager to be highly skilled in their implementation.

New product or service design and development

It is important for a business to be constantly developing new products or services in order to stay ahead of the competition. Planning for new products involves analysis of the existing product portfolio and forecasting the impact of future change. Typical considerations are:
- Can the production methods be more efficient?
- How can productivity be improved?

In a manufacturing business, plant layout may need to change. Some of the features requiring attention might include:
- Is there sufficient working space for the efficient and effective use of production equipment? New arrangements may vary the links between each stage of production and the efficiency of those links.
- How well technology is being implemented? The staff working environment will always be affected by change. The production process could discontinue one style of activity in favour of another, e.g. substituting an assembly line in place of batch processing. This might have positive implications on efficiency, but quality might drop as individuals no longer identify with the quality of their output.
- Are the storage facilities adequate? Changes in operations will invariably highlight deficiencies in infrastructure. They may also make some existing practices redundant, leading to savings.
- Do the changes comply with local, state and federal laws? Sometimes new processes introduce new ways of working, requiring special approval by government to ratify negotiated agreements between employers and employees (as in the mining industry). OH&S compliance will require reassessment in the light of new practices.
- Is the office design/layout efficient and comfortable? For example are the desks and chairs ergonomically correct. Work stations should allow for a smooth flow of people. Is the photocopier located in a convenient position so that staff are not constantly back-tracking. Lunch/tea rooms should be conveniently located and friendly.

In some industries new product design and development leads on to a program of field testing. Models and prototypes are tested see if they work the way the designers expected. In the case of aircraft development or with new pharmaceuticals coming on to the market, the health and safety of potential consumers demands that this process is rigorously carried out at great expense over an extended testing period. The following case studies illustrate this.

Product Development Case Study

Aircraft Testing

This article on aircraft testing and demonstrates the extent to which aircraft manufacturers have to go to ensure the safety of their product before it can go into service.

"For both commercial and military aircraft, flight test preparation begins well before the aircraft is ready to fly. Initially what needs to be tested must be defined, from which the Flight Test Engineers prepare the test plan, which is essentially certain manoeuvres to be flown (or systems to be exercised). A full certification/qualification flight test program for a new aircraft will require testing for many aircraft systems and in-flight regimes; each is typically documented in a separate test plan. During the actual flight testing, similar maneuvers from all test plans are combined and the data collected on the same flights, where practical. This allows the required data to be acquired in the minimum number of flight hours.

Once the flight test data requirements are established, the aircraft is instrumented to record that data for analysis. Typical instrumentation parameters recorded during a flight test are: temperatures, pressures, structural loads, vibration/accelerations, noise levels (interior and exterior), aircraft performance parameters (airspeed, altitude, etc.), aircraft controls positions (stick/yoke position, rudder pedal position, throttle position, etc.), engine performance parameters, and atmospheric conditions. During selected phases of flight test, especially during early development of a new aircraft, many parameters are transmitted to the ground during the flight and monitored by the Flight Test Engineer and test support engineers. This provides for safety monitoring and allows real-time analysis of the data being acquired.

When the aircraft is completely assembled and instrumented, it typically conducts many hours of ground testing before its first/maiden flight. This ground testing will verify basic aircraft systems operations, measure engine performance, evaluate dynamic systems stability, and provide a first look at structural loads. Flight controls will also be checked out. Once all required ground tests are completed, the aircraft is ready for the first flight. First/ maiden flight is a major milestone in any aircraft development program and is undertaken with the utmost caution.

There are several aspects to a flight test program: handling qualities, performance, aero-elastic/flutter stability, avionics/systems capabilities, weapons delivery, and structural loads. Handling qualities evaluates the aircraft's controllability and response to pilot inputs throughout the range of flight. Performance testing evaluates aircraft in relation to its projected abilities, such as speed, range, power available, drag, airflow characteristics, and so forth. Aero-elastic stability evaluates the dynamic response of the aircraft controls and structure to aerodynamic (i.e. air-induced) loads.

Structural tests measure the stresses on the airframe, dynamic components, and controls to verify structural integrity in all flight regimes. Avionics/ systems testing verifies all electronic systems (navigation, communications, radars, sensors, etc.) perform as designed. Weapons delivery looks at the pilot's ability to acquire the target using on-board systems and accurately deliver the ordnance on target. Weapons delivery testing also evaluates the separation of the ordnance as it leaves the aircraft to ensure there are no safety issues. Other military unique tests are: air-to-air refueling, radar/ infrared signature measurement, and aircraft carrier operations. Emergency situations are evaluated as a normal part of all flight test program. Examples are: engine failure during various phases of flight (takeoff, cruise, landing), systems failures, and controls degradation. The overall operations envelope (allowable gross weights, centers-of-gravity, altitude, max/min airspeeds, maneuvers, etc.) is established and verified during flight testing.

Aircraft are always demonstrated to be safe beyond the limits allowed for normal operations in the Flight Manual.

Because the primary goal of a flight test program is to gather accurate engineering data, often on a design that is not fully proven, piloting a flight test aircraft requires a high degree of training and skill, so such programs are typically flown by a specially trained test pilot, and the data is gathered by a flight test engineer, and often visually displayed to the test pilot and/or flight test engineer using flight test instrumentation.

It includes the analysis of a flight for certification. It analyzes the internal and outer part of the flight by checking its all minute parts. Reporting includes the analyzed data result.

The make-up of the Flight Test Team will vary with the organization and complexity of the flight test program, however, there are some key players who are generally part of all flight test organizations. The leader of a flight test team is usually a flight test engineer (FTE) or possibly an experimental test pilot. Other FTEs or pilots could also be involved. Other team members would be the Flight Test Instrumentation Engineer, Instrumentation System Technicians, the aircraft maintenance department (mechanics, electricals, avionics technicians, etc.), Quality/Product Assurance Inspectors, the ground-based computing/data center personnel, plus logistics and administrative support. Engineers from various other disciplines would support the testing of their particular systems and analyze the data acquired for their specialty area.

Since many aircraft development programs are sponsored by government military services, military or government-employed civilian pilots and engineers are often integrated into the flight test team. The government representatives provide program oversight and review and approve data. Government test pilots may also participate in the actual test flights, possibly even on the first/maiden flight."

Source: Wikipedia

Product Development Case Study

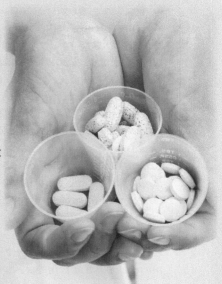

The development of new medicines is carried out under highly regulated conditions. Extensive testing involving clinical trials are required to ensure new drugs have limited side effects and their use is safe for human consumption. The US Federal Drug Administration (FDA) is regarded as a world class authority on drug testing. Acceptance by the FDA is generally regarded as a sufficient standard to be attained by drug manufacturers to ensure that most health jurisdictions in the world will allow the drug to be used.

The article following sets out the tests that a new drug needs to pass before acceptance by the FDA.

Drug Development

It takes on average about 12 - 15 years to develop a drug from an idea through to a product that can be sold for use in patients. A little more than half of this time is spent testing the drug in the laboratory (known as 'pre-clinical' testing). The remainder is spent testing the product in humans (known as 'clinical' testing) and having the data reviewed by the regulatory authorities.

Preclinical Testing

The first step normally involves testing the new drug in the test tube with animal and human cells. These tests help confirm that the drug has the type of effect on cells that might be helpful in treating the target disease. They also help provide an understanding of how the drug might work in the body. The second step normally involves testing the new drug in animals that display a similar disease to the target disease in humans. The purpose of these studies is twofold - to confirm that the drug works and to establish the drug's harmful side-effects. Before moving onto testing in humans, various other steps are required such as:

- *being able to manufacture the drug so that the product is completely standardised;*

- *determining the best way to administer the drug; and*

- *knowing what happens to the drug in the body.*

Clinical Testing

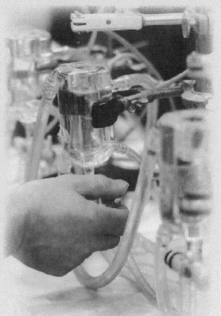

Once the drug is ready to be tested in humans, for registration in the USA an application is made to the Food and Drug Administration (FDA) for permission to carry out such testing. In Australia the regulatory body is the Therapeutic Good Authority (TGA). This is an extensive review process where the FDA considers all the pre-clinical study results are considered to determine whether or not the drug has sufficient merit and safety to warrant being tested in humans. If approved with this process in the USA, the drug is said to have Investigational New Drug (IND) status. An application then is made to the Investigational Review Board or Ethics Committee of a particular hospital or clinic where the study is to be conducted. The study needs to reach certain standards of scientific merit and ethical conduct before being approved. The clinical program then is conducted in a series of steps known broadly as Phase I, II and III.

Phase I

*Phase I clinical trials are mainly intended to answer questions regarding the safety and tolerability of a new drug. It is not usual to look for or even expect any beneficial health outcome of the drug at this stage. In fact, many Phase I studies involve healthy volunteers. A common approach in Phase I is to give the drug to people on the basis of an increasing dosage. The dosage is increased slowly over days or weeks until unwanted side-effects begin to appear. The highest dosage that can reasonably be tolerated is known as the maximum tolerable dose (MTD). Usually the MTD is the maximum dosage selected to be used into later studies. Apart from safety, other matters often studied in Phase I are **bio-availability** and* **pharmacokinetics**:

1. **bio-availability** *refers to the ability to deliver the drug in a usable form to the disease target. Phase I studies are meant to determine whether the drug is best delivered orally, or by injection, or through the skin;*

2. **pharmacokinetics** *refers to the behaviour of the drug in the body. This measures factors such as how long the drug remains in the body, whether the body breaks it down to other compounds and how it leaves the body.*

Phase I studies usually only involve small number of individuals, typically 15-30. Sometimes Phase I testing is divided into two steps known as Phase Ia and Phase Ib. Phase 1a studies normally are conducted as a short-term study to ensure safety before embarking on the longer and more comprehensive Phase Ib study.

Phase II

Phase II clinical trials primarily are intended to demonstrate whether or not the new drug will provide any benefit ('efficacy'), and whether that benefit is sufficiently better than standard treatments to warrant further development. Often a range of dosages is employed to define the best dosage in terms of safety and efficacy to adopt as the final dosage to be tested in later, larger studies. Phase II trials are often placebo-controlled and double-blinded. That is, neither the patient nor their doctor knows whether the patient is receiving the drug or a dummy placebo. Exceptions are life-threatening diseases such as cancer where there is no effective alternative therapy and it would be unethical to offer such patients a placebo treatment, or when the new drug is given in addition to the patient's usual drugs. Phase II patients normally are very carefully selected and must meet certain strict criteria on such things as disease status, age, previous therapies and other diseases and medications. For cancer therapies Phase II studies typically involve 50-200 patients and take 18-24 months to complete.

Phase III

The drug will only progress to a Phase III study if there is sufficient evidence from the Phase II study of clinical benefit and safety. The primary purpose of a Phase III study is to evaluate the benefit of a new drug under real-life conditions. Phase III studies usually are conducted in a number of different hospitals and clinics to ensure a range of operating conditions. Phase III studies usually are placebo-controlled and double-blinded and can involve hundreds or even thousands of patients. As a general rule, the number of patients is a function of how more beneficial a new drug is compared to standards therapies - the smaller the benefit, the greater the number of patients. Testing under 'real life' conditions in larger numbers of patients provides the opportunity to observe any rare side effects of treatment or possible interactions with other treatments.

Regulatory Approval/Phase IV

The results from all the Phase I, II and III studies are submitted to the FDA (in the USA) and other regulatory authorities in other territories for review. If the regulators agree that the data proves the efficacy and safety of the drug, and that it provides sufficient benefit over existing therapies, then the drug is granted New Drug Approval (NDA) status and can be marketed. Once a drug is on the market and freely available, the Company is required to maintain a constant watch for adverse events and to report these to the FDA. This ongoing review is known as Phase IV.

Some facts about drug development

Companies are bound by a number of constraints during drug development: companies are forbidden by the FDA to make unsubstantiated claims about the product. Until the new drug is approved by the FDA for a particular purpose, the Company cannot make any reference to its likely benefit to patients, companies are unable to discuss clinical trial results during a trial. Novogen conducts its clinical trials in accordance with international guidelines and these guidelines are intended to protect the privacy of individual patients and the integrity of the trial. Generally, this means that Novogen cannot divulge any results until the trial is completed. Also, while Novogen is the Sponsor of its different clinical trials, they are conducted under the auspices of hospitals and clinics who under the terms of the contract have total responsibility for announcing any results, recruitment of trials. Novogen is unable to participate in recruitment of subjects to its clinical trials. This responsibility is borne entirely by the hospitals and clinics running the trials.

Source: (Novogen web site)

Supply chain management (SCM)

SCM represents an approach to business which is output or customer centred as opposed to input or production based.

Elements of an SCM organisation are:
- Strategy development; including operational procedures designed to produce outputs consistent with customer demands.
- Planning. Starting with the customer need, the planning process drives down into the organisation, shaping product design, production planning, facilities planning, and resources to ensure the whole business is oriented towards meeting customer demand.
- Logistics: internal and external transport and distribution resources.
- Procurement: obtaining raw materials necessary to create required products demanded by customers.
- Product Lifecycle Management: This refers to research and development, product design and replacement to satisfy changing consumer demand.
- Efficient operation of the different divisions of a business involved in meeting customer demand.
- Management of plant and equipment to ensure they are applied to meeting customer needs.

Linfox is a large Australian Company involved in Supply Chain Management.

Logistics

Logistics is concerned with ensuring that each stage of the supply chain comes together in the most efficient way possible. Logistics management may be part of the business, or the function could be met by a contracting Logistics company. The role of Logistics management includes:
- storage of finished goods in a strategically placed warehouse
- receiving orders directly from customers, or from the sales department of the supplier
- invoicing and despatching orders to customers
- delivery of orders on time
- transport bulk goods between storage centres
- inventory forecasting ordering and receiving.

" E-quik" specialises in supply chain logistics.

e-Quik is an integrated order processing service that operates under a 'Same Day' Order In/Order Out protocol. In short, that means that orders can be received, picked, packed and despatched to your client all in the same day.

Whether you're in business-to-business or business-to-consumer manufacturing or marketing, e-Quik can help you do what you do best – by warehousing your inventory and relieving you of day-to-day logistics and distribution hassles.
- e-Quik can remotely receive orders direct from you, your branch network or your customers direct.
- e-Quik manages your inventory, enabling fast and efficient picking (and re-ordering).
- e-Quik can handle a wide variety of packing requirements. from the very fragile, to the very heavy. to the very large.
- e-Quik intelligently aggregates your orders, providing the most cost-effective despatch solutions for you.

Developed by Coghlan Pty Ltd, e-Quik is the result of over 20 years of experience providing order fulfilment services to the Australasian market. It's valuable experience that has built confidence and trust among Coghlan's clients – as well as a reputation for reliability.

www.equikfulfilment.com.au

e-commerce

e-commerce (electronic commerce) refers to buying, selling and paying for products over the internet. The customer doesn't directly see the product or seller. The transaction is carried out electronically. The advent of e-commerce has made supply chain management and logistics much more efficient due to the fact that buyers and sellers and their channels of communication are greatly improved. Communication occurs via email and websites and goods are paid for by electronic funds transfer (EFT):

In recent times we have seen an increase in e-commerce as people become more confident with purchasing a product from an overseas country online. Traditional retailers in Australia complain that international sellers using e-commerce are competing unfairly. There is no mechanism to collect the GST from online sellers. Gerry Harvey has been an outspoken critic of e-commerce for a number of reasons, but has recently reconsidered his position:

> *Harvey Norman considers e-commerce*
>
> *Mr Harvey confirmed yesterday that he is still exploring the possibility of establishing his own on-line shopping operation based out of China.*
> *But that doesn't mean they are going to be directly competing against their own franchisees. If Harvey Norman Holdings Ltd sell online from China into Australia they will be selling to a different customer than the one who walks into Harvey Norman, Domayne and Joyce Mayne franchises.*
> *He understands that buyer behaviour is not binary and that the people who shop online are a different customer to the one his franchisees are likely to sell their wares.*
> *He knows that the customer who buys a chair from LifeInteriors.com.au are not lost sales in a Harvey Norman franchise. They are different customers in different contexts. One is walking through a store because they want to experience a tactile product and ask questions--the other is shopping for convenience or bargains online.*
> *What international traders (and Australian traders selling overseas) call these taxes are protectionist trade barriers. Tariff and non-tariff barriers are generally frowned upon and there is immense global pressure to remove these barriers to provide free trade opportunities.*

An important factor relating to e-commerce are the **social responsibilities** relating to this form of commercial activity. There must be a great deal of trust between seller and customer in terms of the description of products and also through the payment for the products. In other words, the product must match its description. Secondly, there have been problems of security in relation to payment via credit card.

It must be said, however, that e-commerce is the way of the future and will only expand in the years ahead.

Global sourcing

Global sourcing refers to the action of a business sourcing its raw materials from anywhere in the world. It is done for several reasons;

- overseas sources are often cheaper
- bulk supply from an overseas source may be more convenient
- the security of delivery of raw materials is of prime importance.

Globalisation has led to vertical integration of business i.e. an oil company which owns the oil tankers, owns the oil refineries and owns the service stations. As globalisation has proceeded, vertical integration has accelerated.

In the same way local manufacturers have to decide whether or not to produce components that go into their products or purchase them from overseas. This concept has been made more attractive through the standardisation of components. It is not uncommon for different car manufacturers to use identical components.

Outsourcing

A business may contract certain work "out" to professionals such as lawyers and accountants. Many smaller businesses have neither the size or financial capacity to employ any of these professionals on a full time basis.

Recently there has been a trend for businesses of all sizes to outsource much of their work in order to access the best talent available. They may also do this to save money. For example there are many companies contracting out their manufacturing processes to contractors all around the world who assemble the components and then sell them under a brand name. The Apple computer company doesn't assemble its own computers but instead contracts out its computer assembly functions. Indeed this technique of contract manufacturing is common in the information technology and motor vehicle industries.

Businesses of all sizes and functions outsource. Many people think that only small businesses outsource because they are not big enough to have say a HR department, an IT department, a publications department, an accounting department, a marketing department and an operations department etc. This is clearly not the case. Large businesses outsource as well, as the Apple example above demonstrates.

With regard to advantages and disadvantages of outsourcing like many things in Business Studies there is no right or wrong answer, only two ways of looking at the problem. Some firms may find it convenient to outsource and others prefer to carry out their operations in-house, depending on the nature of the business and circumstances. As a student you only need to be aware of the two positions and be able to comment on them.

Advantages of Outsourcing

The advantages of outsourcing include bringing in specialist skills, cost factors, efficiency of production and flexibility of delivery. Often the business owner doesn't possess the necessary skills to manage certain aspects of the business. For example they may not have any accounting skills, so this has to be outsourced.

- It is often cheaper to outsource certain functions to specific experts. If the business had to gear up to perform certain specialist tasks themselves, it could be quite expensive.
- Specialist firms are usually more efficient at carrying out certain tasks than generalist firms.
- Outsourcing can provide flexibility of delivery rather than waiting for a division of the business to produce a certain component that they are not geared up to produce.

Disadvantages of Outsourcing

The arguments against outsourcing include:

- businesses may lose some control over the production process.
- they may find that they are not able to control delivery times or avoid industrial disputes in the supplier company.
- Quality control might also be an issue that can't be controlled and needs to be addressed. In the recent QANTAS industrial dispute, the unions argued that maintenance outsourced to overseas providers was substandard. They argued that overseas standards were too low, and the QANTAS safety record was put at risk.

A business decision to engage in outsourcing is neither right nor wrong. It is important to understand the arguments for and against.

Technology

Businesses need to use state of the art technology as part of their **operations strategies.** The pace of technological change is constantly accelerating, and business must keep up with this change in order to survive in the 21st Century. Computerisation has led to the technological revolution in business through such things as computer assisted design (CAD) and the introduction of robotics into production.

New information and communications technologies are major influences on business both domestically and globally. The cost of global communication is declining. The internet, mobile phones and electronic funds transfer are opening up the global market. Technology is allowing businesses of all sizes to move from domestic to international markets. Consumers can purchase products from anywhere in the world on the internet. The internet also opens the door for innovative producers to reach a much larger market place and take advantage of much larger economies of scale. Indeed, even now consumers are able to just as readily look at shopping catalogues on the internet as those delivered to their letter boxes at home.

Technology shortens the production process and keeps costs down. It allows the business to access more markets for raw materials and customers through information technology.

More and more businesses are using websites to inform customers about their products and sell those products on-line. Even the simple use of email and teleconferencing has become a normal part of doing business on a day-to-day basis.

Leading Edge Technology

The pace of change introducing new ways of using the internet, mobile communications and systems to transfer funds has accelerated. These leading edge technologies assist business to operate at increasing levels of efficiency. They:

- allow business to access business information and customers all around the world
- allow contact between businesses anywhere in the world at any time of the day or night
- allow businesses to move funds anywhere around the world instantly in order to conduct that business through electronic funds transfer (EFT)
- allow any individual to work for any company in the world without leaving home. This is known as Tele-migration
- allow international delivery services, including door-to-door delivery of any size consignment which has already been cleared by customs through a process known as electronic data exchange. This allows any business to sell directly to any other business and bypass many levels of distribution
- allow international finance services,like "international non-recourse factoring" that allows business to sell anywhere in the world without a bad debt risk
- allow "electronic clustering" which enables clusters of companies anywhere in the world to share information and resources and develop personal business relationships
- allow "electronic outsourcing" which makes the provision of specialist services inexpensive, convenient and practical. This allows individual enterprises to concentrate their efforts and resources into their areas of expertise
- allow what is known as "fractional distillation of information" which taps the world's reservoir of information, distills and analyses its contents and provides a business with specific information quickly and accurately.

Another leading edge technology available to business is automation and the use of **robotics**. The car assembly industry uses robots to perform repetitive tasks. They can also be used in situations where the production process is dangerous such as with the handling of chemicals or radio-active material. Robots can work continuously for days and don't require rest breaks, thus speeding up the production process.

Established Technology

In the 21st century we need to consider some of the **established** technology that we take for granted. Some of this technology has only emerged in the last 20 years but is now well established. Examples of these technologies are

- mobile phones
- fax machines
- ATMs
- photo copiers/scanners
- internet
- bar coding of stock.

Established technologies have improved our access to customers and suppliers like never before. They have become part of our **operations strategies.**

Inventory management

A business needs a supply of raw materials to make sure it is able to maintain a smooth production process. Sometimes there is a lead time associated with the acquisition of raw materials so it is necessary to keep extra stock on hand. A business will also keep some finished goods in stock to enable customers to be supplied promptly. Inventory management is therefore a very important aspect of **operations**

Advantages and Disadvantages of holding stock.

In today's world, businesses must decide how much stock to hold at any one time. If too much stock is held then money is tied up reducing liquidity. On the other hand if too little stock is held then the business risks running out of stock. There is no clear answer to this dilemma and the business manager must decide on the best plan for their particular business based on experience and sometimes even gut feeling. Business people are not perfect and sometimes mistakes are made.

With perishable goods such as fruit and vegetables, the fruit vendor, delicatessen or restaurant owner risks making a loss if they buy too much stock. Overstocks will need to be thrown out when it goes bad. Purchasing is a critical function where experience plays a major role. Not enough stock will reduce sales; too much stock will result in waste, and consequential losses.

When exercising control over inventory, a manager will need to ask the following questions:

- Is there sufficient inventory (stock) on hand to meet the demands of customers or the production process? One should realise that inventory is not always there as a saleable item. Inventory might be stocks of raw materials to be used in the production process. The business must ensure that the right quantity of stock is being held. This is where Just-In-Time (JIT) stock management comes in handy.
- Is the cost of transporting these inventories reasonable?
- Is the inventory adequately insured while being stored or transported? A flood or fire could wipe a business out if the inventory is valuable and uninsured.
- Is security adequate? Theft of inventory by customers or staff can be very expensive to the business. The business can control this by using video surveillance, dyes, security tags, magnetic strips or bag searches. However this last one has to be done with a great deal of discretion.
- Is wastage being kept to a minimum?
- Is the inventory being turned over quickly enough so that some stock is not becoming obsolete or out of date?
- Is the business using the most efficient storage methods?
- Are the stocktaking procedures efficient?

LIFO and FIFO

Inventory valuation may be determined in a number of different ways:

- LIFO (Last in First Out) Inventory is valued by using the last cost when calculating cost of goods sold (COGS).
- FIFO (First in First Out) Inventory is valued by using historical cost when calculating COGS.
- Specific identification: The actual cost of items sold is used to calculate COGS. This method is used for high value items.
- Average Cost: An average cost of the total inventory is used for COGS. This method is widely used in small businesses.

If a business used a cash accounting system, inventory valuation methods are irrelevant for calculating COGS. The expenses are incurred when goods are paid for and not identified when making sales.

For accrual accounting systems, the cost of inventory is more related to sales. A business is able to use LIFO to minimise tax in an inflationary period. A side affect of this method is that inventory may be valued at less than market price. If there is a significant increase in prices, a business would revalue its assets, reporting this as income. As a consequence, prior tax minimisation would be reversed.

If a business values assets using FIFO, in an inflationary environment the value of inventory will steadily increase. Revaluing of inventory will not be necessary as the value of stock will oscillate allowing report cost.

Just in Time (JIT)

JIT inventory management is an operating policy used by business to optimise inventory costs. Raw materials, work in progress, finished goods and goods in transit inventories are all maintained at just above minimum levels. It is important not to run out of stock because this may interrupt production (raw material shortages) or cause a loss of sales(finished goods shortages).

Having excess inventory is costly: too much stock places increased demands on working capital. The cost of storing large amounts of stock can be quite significant. The business is also exposed to increased risks and the costs of associated insurance cover.

JIT systems were initially introduced in the motor vehicle assembly industry. Parts manufacturers were contracted to supply components according to assembly line schedules drawn up by the vehicle manufacturer. Components would be incorporated into vehicles within a few days of their initial manufacture and supply. Neither party held significant stocks of components as the supply contracts required delivery to be "just in time".

The practice has spread to the wider business community. With the introduction of digital printing, many school textbooks are no longer produced in large print runs. Textbook printing (including this textbook) is carried out "just in time".

JIT systems also apply to distribution. A retailer may accept an order for a product and then quickly obtain supply from the manufacturer. With email ordering and overnight transport, the goods may be in the store the next day.

Other than expenses, the level of inventories held by a business will also depend on:
- the levels of stock required to run the business smoothly.
- the reliability and frequency of deliveries.
- the types of product. If a product is perishable then only small stocks will be held. The same holds true if the product is a seasonal one such as a fashion item.
- insurance and security considerations are also important. Inventory that is expensive to insure or has the potential for theft will be kept in smaller quantities.
- the efficiency of the control process i.e. the responsiveness of the business in ordering or acquiring new stock.

Quality management

Quality management is a continuously cyclical process involving **control, quality assurance** and **improvement.** Managers exercise control over process, supervising and directing staff and technology in operations. Assurance refers to monitoring and measurement of output at strategic points in the operations process. Improvement follows as corrective action arising from quality assurance is implemented. Effective managers promote quality by applying

- entrepreneurial flair
- innovative skills
- experience
- people management skills
- decision making skills.
- communication skills.

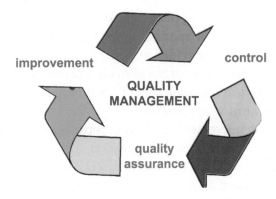

Control

Management control systems gather and use information to evaluate the performance of different parts of a business. They could be applied to human, physical and financial resources. These systems help the business to implement its strategies.

One of the most widely used procedures for providing management information about the storage, transfer and disposition of business data is the use of barcodes. Retail stores record stock receiving, storage and sale of inventory by the use of barcode scanners. Postal and transport services use barcodes to monitor delivery and accounting of consignments. Operations control systems use barcodes to report on raw materials, work in progress and finished goods.

Management control systems such as barcodes, help businesses implement strategies providing information about the storage, transfer and disposition of data.

Some applications of barcodes are listed below:

- Almost every item other than fresh produce from a grocery store, department store, and mass merchandiser has a UPC barcode on it. This helps track items and also reduces instances of shoplifting involving price tag swapping, although shoplifters can now print their own barcodes.
- Barcodes are widely used in shop floor control applications software where employees can scan work orders and track the time spent on a job.
- Barcodes can be used to carry out an accurate stock-take.
- Barcodes can be used to reduce theft.
- Retail chain membership cards (issued mostly by grocery stores and specialty "big box" retail stores such as sporting equipment, office supply, or pet stores) use bar codes to uniquely identify a consumer. Retailers can offer customized marketing and greater understanding of individual consumer shopping patterns. At the point of sale, shoppers can get product discounts or special marketing offers through the address or e-mail address provided at registration.
- Document Management tools often allow for barcoded sheets to facilitate the separation and indexing of documents that have been imaged in batch scanning applications.
- The tracking of item movement, including rental cars, airline luggage, nuclear waste, mail, express mail and parcels.
- Since 2005, airlines use an IATA-standard 2D barcode on boarding passes (BCBP), and since 2008 2D barcodes sent to mobile phones enable electronic boarding passes.
- Barcoded entertainment event tickets allow the holder to enter sports arenas, cinemas, theatres, fairgrounds, transportation, etc. This can allow the proprietor to identify duplicate or fraudulent tickets more easily.
- They can track the arrival and departure of vehicles from rental facilities.
- Barcodes can integrate with in-motion checkweighers to identify the item being weighed in a conveyor line for data collection.
- Some 2D barcodes embed a hyperlink to a web page. A capable mobile phone might be used to read the barcode and browse the linked website, which can help a shopper find the best price for an item in the vicinity.
- The 1991 Barcode Battler computer game system, used any standard barcode to generate combat statistics.
- Today, barcodes are issued by GS1, the most widely used supply chain standards system in the world.

Using Barcodes to Track, Trace and Manage

"A barcode is an optical machine-readable representation of data, which shows data about the object to which it attaches. Originally, barcodes represented data by varying the widths and spacing of parallel lines, and may be referred to as linear or 1 dimensional (1D). Later they evolved into rectangles, dots, hexagons and other geometric patterns in 2 dimensions (2D). Although 2D systems use a variety of symbols, they are generally referred to as barcodes as well. Barcodes originally were scanned by special–optical scanners called barcode readers, scanners and interpretive software are available on devices including desktop printers and smart phones.

The first use of barcodes was to label railroad cars, but they were not commercially successful until they were used to automate supermarket checkout systems, a task for which they have become almost universal. Their use has spread to many other tasks that are generically referred to as Auto ID Data Capture (AIDC). Other systems are attempting to make inroads in the AIDC market, but the simplicity, universality and low cost of barcodes has limited the role of these other systems."

Wikepedia

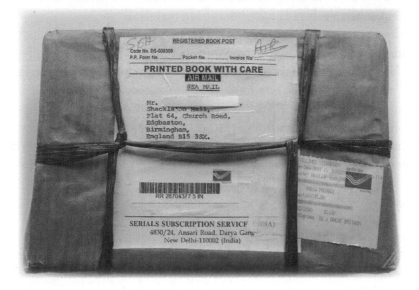

Assurance(quality assurance)

A quality assurance manager is expected to monitor the efficiency of business operations. They may use *industrial engineering* methods, such as *time-and-motion* studies, to measure performance and outputs.

The QA manager's role is to count, measure and report on all aspects of operations to enable the line manager to direct and supervise. QA reports will highlight any deviation from planned or standard performance and suggest what corrective action needs to be taken.

There are a number of recognised quality assurance policies used in business including:

- Inspection of output at each stage of the process to ensure that this output reaches the required standards for further processing or sale to the customer. In many situations it is not possible to inspect every item so in this case random inspections may be carried out and if the operations process is identical for each item then it can be assumed the whole batch will be up to the standard required.
- World's best practice is a policy adopted by business to apply and adapt the best methods and practices from around the world. For example, international standards must be applied to components going into a car that is manufactured in Australia. The part may be made in Malaysia but the quality of that part must be of the same quality as if it had it been made here in Australia. Otherwise the overall quality of the car will be inferior, especially if that component consistently fails once it has been installed.
- World's best practice is becoming more and more common in other industries. With most of the world's largest companies sending their production off shore, the standard of output must be the same as if the product was made in Japan, USA or Australia.
- Total Quality Management (TQM) is a concept in business where all employees are involved in programs to achieve the best possible standards of quality throughout all aspects of the business. Devised by an American, it was first implemented in Japan and has now become accepted and adapted worldwide.

Improvement

Quality management assists line management to take control of business operations. Quality assurance provides information to enable effective management decisions to be taken. From this position of strength, it is possible for improvement to take place. Quality Circles and Kaizen are devices used by business to promote continuous improvement.

- Quality Circles comprise groups of skilled employees gathered together in a process that aims to better the quality of a product/service or procedure that will benefit a customer or the business by decreasing unnecessary costs.
- Kaizen is the Japanese concept of constantly seeking improvement and questioning current methods of production. Workers work on achieving higher standards and improving the way they do things.

Overcoming resistance to change

Change is an important element in business improvement. Resistance to change is quite common. Many business managers feel that if a procedure is working well enough, then why change. However, well enough is not always good enough and better, more efficient procedures can be found. There are several reasons for resistance to change.

Financial costs

The first of these is the cost of **purchasing new equipment**. In a climate of accelerating technology, new equipment such as computerised machinery can be expensive. This reason for resistance to change is more common in the small business area, rather than the large business because of the financial constraints that small business has. For example, a large business such as an insurance company has the financial capacity to easily purchase new equipment to upgrade its services. However a small business either cannot afford to do this or must upgrade slowly- over a number of years.

Redundancy payments

Redundancy payments are also a considerable expense for a business considering change. A person becomes redundant when the job he/she was doing no longer exists or when an employer doesn't require the employee any longer. Any redundancy payout is an expense of implementing a change. The size of these payments is determined by law. The formula may be complex, but in general terms it relates to the number of years of service the employee has had with the company and what their salary was at the time of redundancy.

Once an employee who has been made redundant leaves their employment and a termination payment must be organised. Workers are compensated for losing their job and for the emotional stress that may be caused, particularly when an employee has been working for a company for a long period of time.

With voluntary separation the employer has to calculate entitlements such as holiday pay and long service pay. These payments are usually made on the last day of service.

With involuntary separation, there may be additional payments required. Sometimes these may be the result of industrial agreements influenced by the government, unions and employers.

Either way, the costs involved with the redundancy payments are considerable and are often resisted by employers.

Retraining

Retraining can also be an expensive deterrent to change in business. When businesses undertake change, staff often need to be retrained to use new equipment and learn new methodologies.

The aircraft industry uses flight simulators to train pilots. Pilots need to be familiar with:
- landing in every airport in the world
- how weather affects flight safety.

In all cases training is a necessary part of change in business. Some aspects of training are more expensive than others. It is the dynamic managers who take advantage of training- usually to the benefit of their businesses in the long run, because their employees are then at the forefront of their industry through this training.

Reorganising Plant Layouts

The costs involved in **reorganising plant layout** can also be considerable. This reorganisation may mean major changes to buildings and facilities. Physical change is often resisted by employees in their comfort zone. Either way these changes are expensive and are a source of resistance to change by managers.

Inertia of owners and managers

Many owners and managers don't want to change what they have been doing for years, citing the "If it ain't broke, don't try to fix it" concept. They are happy making normal profits without extending themselves. However in the long run, change will catch up to them and they will be forced to change their equipment and systems otherwise they will eventually go out of business as their more dynamic competitors develop more efficient production methods.

Global factors

The global business of today is living in a completely different world to that of the global business of 20 years ago and the main element in this change scenario is technology.

Twenty years ago, businesses sourced their raw materials locally or from a limited number of overseas suppliers. They didn't have access to a multiplicity of suppliers through the internet. Globalisation has led to vertical integration of business e.g. an oil company may own the oil tankers, the oil refineries and the service stations. As globalisation has accelerated, vertical integration has become more common.

Global Sourcing

Global sourcing is a term used to describe the practice of *sourcing* raw materials from the global market for goods and services across geopolitical boundaries. Global sourcing attempts to exploit global efficiencies in the delivery of a product or service. These efficiencies include low cost skilled labour, low cost raw materials and other economic factors like tax breaks and low trade tariffs. By doing this the business keeps the costs of its operations down.

Common examples of globally-sourced products or services include:
- labour-intensive manufactured products produced in Asia
- call centre staff in the Philippines and India are paid at local rates
- IT work performed by programmers in India and Eastern Europe is much cheaper than the local IT work.

While these are examples of low-cost sourcing, global sourcing is not limited to low-cost countries.

The majority of companies today strive to harness the potential of global sourcing in reducing cost. Hence it is commonly found that global sourcing initiatives and programs form an integral part of what is known as the strategic sourcing plan and procurement strategy of many multinational companies.

The global sourcing of goods and services has advantages and disadvantages that can go beyond the concept of low cost to the business. Some advantages of global sourcing, beyond low cost, include:
- learning how to do business in a potential market
- tapping into skills or resources unavailable domestically
- developing alternate supplier sources to stimulate competition which might increase supply availability.

Some key disadvantages of global sourcing can include:
- the hidden costs associated with different cultures and time zones
- exposure to financial and political risks in countries with (often) emerging economies. This can occur through fraud or in payment situations where the business person hasn't done business in that country before.
- increased risk of the loss of intellectual property, and increased monitoring costs relative to domestic supply
- long lead times
- the risk of port shutdowns interrupting supply
- the difficulty of monitoring product quality.

Multinationals may outsource their global sourcing administration. They may use an International Procurement Organisations (IPO) These IPOs take primary responsibility for identifying and developing key suppliers across the globe and help satisfy the sourcing requirements of the client. Such arrangements facilitate country-based sourcing efforts. In large and complex economies, such as China, where a range of sub-*markets* exist and suppliers span the entire value chain of a product/commodity. IPOs provide essential on-the-ground information.

Local manufacturers have to decide whether or not to produce components that go into their products or purchase them from overseas.

Economies of scale

Economies of scale is the **lowering of the unit cost of production** by spreading costs over a larger output. As companies become larger and begin to trade overseas, many will set up offices, research and production facilities overseas. They can access information and technology not always available in Australia. They also have access to cheap labour if they set up branch offices and production facilities in countries such as those in South East Asia. Economies of scale will often occur, for example, through the production of different parts of a car in different countries according to where each component can be made most cheaply. The car will then be assembled where the largest market is, so avoiding the higher costs involved in transporting the completed unit.

To accommodate economies of scale a multinational corporation will often acquire a business in a foreign country to control the supply of it's raw materials. Equally, a commodities trader may acquire mining leases or purchase sugar, coffee, or cocoa plantations in developing countries to ensure supply and/or to take advantage of the **economies of scale** provided by vertical integration.

The trader might ultimately own:
- all the processes of production
- the transportation processes
- processing plant
- retail outlets.

Scanning and learning

To be effective, a business must be aware of its operating environment and if proposing to undertake new activities, it is necessary to scan the new market environment before proceeding. Having gathered the necessary intelligence, the business should develop and learn new skills.

Scanning in this context may be directed towards:
- Demographics
  - Economic factors
  - The natural environment
  - Technological influences
- Sociocultural factors
  - Political trends
  - Ethnic differences
  - Legal conditions

Ignoring these trends, or simply not experiencing them may be critical to the success of a business as it proceeds. Technology and fashion could determine the success of new products. Failure to scan for changes in the business environment and learn how to cater for these changes could have negative results.

Business must also monitor (scan) significant business factors such as customers, competitors, suppliers, distributors and dealers that might affect its ability to earn profits. The business unit should set up a marketing intelligence system to track trends and important developments. For each trend or development. Management needs to identify the associated opportunities and threats. There are three ways of scanning the business environment:
- ad-hoc scanning i.e. short term, infrequent examinations usually initiated by a crisis.
- regular scanning- studies done on a regular schedule (e.g. once a year).
- continuous scanning - continuous structured data collection and processing on a broad range of environmental factors will enable a business to continuously revise its actions.

Most business people feel that in today's turbulent business environment the best scanning method available is continuous scanning. The firm can act quickly, take advantage of opportunities before competitors do and respond to environmental threats before significant damage is done to their business.

Learning can be single loop or double loop. Single loop learning results in minor adjustments in the business strategy as a response to the scanning without changing the basic way the company does business. Double loop learning results in radical changes in the way the company does business. The business could break out of existing thought patterns and to create a new mindset.

Effective use of scanning and learning strategies will keep the business at the cutting edge.

Research and development

According to the *Organization for Economic Co-operation and Development (OECD)* Research and Development refers to "creative work undertaken on a systematic basis in order to increase the stock of knowledge, including knowledge of man, culture and society, and the use of this stock of knowledge to devise new applications".

Business undertakes research and development to discover newer and better ways of doing things. Australian Governments have subsidised R&D as outlined below:

Research and Development and Australian Business.

Australia's strong business performance in recent years has been underpinned by a record of innovation and a long standing commitment to research and development (R&D), aimed at increasing productivity, building new markets and boosting international competitiveness. Australian governments, private enterprise and research institutions are firmly committed to supporting Australian innovation and excellence.

According to the Australian Bureau of Statistics, business spending on R&D totalled $10.1 billion in 2005–06, an increase of 11.8 per cent in real terms over the previous year. The major contributors were manufacturing ($3.9 billion), property and business services ($1.7 billion) and mining industries (also $1.7 billion).

The mining industry reported the biggest growth in R&D spending, increasing by $417.2 million (33 per cent) in 2005–06 compared to the previous year. Although Australia's R&D expenditure as a proportion of gross domestic product remains lower than the OECD average, Australia's spending has increased for the past seven successive years.

More than 119,000 Australians were employed full-time in R&D activities in 2004–05. This is measured in person years of effort, where one person year of effort is equal to a full-time employee whose time is entirely devoted to R&D for a whole year. The Australian Government supports R&D through direct funding as well as providing significant tax concessions to encourage private sector investment.

The Australian Government allows companies to deduct 125 per cent of eligible expenditure incurred on R&D activities when they lodge their corporate tax returns. In some circumstances, the tax offset for a portion of their spending may be increased to 175 per cent. The R&D tax offset also allows eligible small companies to 'cash out' their R&D tax losses. At June 2007, more than 6295 companies with a reported R&D expenditure of around $9.2 billion were registered for the tax concessions.

In May 2007, the Australian Government further boosted R&D investment with a 10-year, $1.4 billion package to help Australian industries become more internationally competitive and sustainable. The package included the provision of $500 million to extend eligibility for the premium 175 per cent tax concessions for R&D projects undertaken in Australia, regardless of whether the intellectual property is held overseas or in Australia.

The Australian Government also provided $200 million a year for the Commercial Ready program, which was introduced in 2005 to provide matching grants to small to medium-sized businesses for R&D activities with a high commercial potential, proof-of-concept activities, and early stage commercialisation. An additional $90.3 million over 10 years was allocated in 2007 for Commercial Ready Plus to provide matching grants to small to medium-sized enterprises and spin-offs from universities and public sector research organisations through a faster and simpler application process.

Priority areas

R&D priority areas include information and communications technology (ICT), biotechnology, manufacturing, mining and the food industry.

The Australian Government has committed $380 million over 10 years to 2011 to a centre of excellence for ICT research, research training and commercialisation. The centre, known as National ICT Australia (NICTA), was established in 2002 as an independent, not-for-profit company. NICTA is now one of Australia's largest ICT research organisations, employing more than 300 research and support staff and around 260 postgraduate students.

In 2000, the Australian Government launched a National Biotechnology Strategy, which was strengthened in 2004. The strategy is designed to enable government and key stakeholders to work together to ensure that developments in biotechnology are harnessed for the benefit of the Australian community, industry and the environment and to strengthen Australia's competitiveness in biotechnology.

In the food sector, the Australian Government is providing $54.2 million over four years from 2007 for R&D activities to further improve the food industry's export competitiveness.

The Australian Government has also awarded $36.2 million to the Commonwealth Scientific and Industrial Research Organisation (CSIRO) to support the development of niche manufacturing businesses based on nanotechnology through the creation of a new National Research Flagship.

Research and development capability

Australia has a strong research and development capability. There are about 50 000 people in higher education organisations who are involved in R&D, another 36 000 in the business sector and 19 000 in federal and state government agencies and laboratories. Each year about 16 000 science students and 9000 engineering students graduate from Australia's 39 universities.

CSIRO is the biggest government R&D agency in Australia. Founded in 1926, it is one of the world's largest and most diverse research institutions. Its staff of about 6500 includes 4000 scientists and other researchers working in more than 50 laboratories and field stations in Australia and overseas. Their research covers agribusiness, information technology, manufacturing, health, sustainable energy, mining and minerals, space, the environment and natural resources. Internationally, CSIRO is involved in more than 740 research activities with scientific organisations and agencies in more than 80 countries.

Since 2003, CSIRO's National Research Flagship program has been developing large-scale collaborations to address national challenges in climate, energy, food, light metals, health, minerals, manufacturing, water and oceans.

Cooperative research centres

The cooperative research centre (CRC) program is an Australian Government-funded initiative to enhance collaboration between business and researchers. The program was established in 1990 with the aim of turning Australia's scientific innovations into successful new products, services and technologies, making our industries more efficient, productive and competitive. Participants include private sector organisations (both large and small enterprises), industry associations, universities and government research agencies.

CSIRO is the biggest single participant in the program, providing staff and other resources to nearly 40 CRCs in 2006. The Australian Government has directly committed more than $2 billion to the program since its establishment and CSIRO has committed $1 billion.

The Australian Government grants awards of between $20 million and $40 million to CRCs over a seven-year project period. This funding must be matched by cash and/or in-kind contributions, such as expertise and research facilities. Since the program's inception, the government has funded 158 CRCs. The program currently has a network of around 70 CRCs.

The CRCs cover six broad sectors:
- *agriculture and rural-based manufacturing*
- *environment*
- *information and communications technology*
- *manufacturing technology*
- *medical science and technology*
- *mining and energy*
- *Since 1990, CRCs have taken out more than 2600 patents in Australia and 3400 overseas.*

Some recent CRC successes include:
- *a new test for avian influenza that has been trialled in nine veterinary laboratories in Australia and New Zealand*
- *a new electronic train-braking system that will contribute significantly to the safety of the rail industry and could deliver $1.6 billion in benefits to the industry over the next 15 years*
- *an irrigation package that provides a framework and process for assessing the economic, social and environmental aspects of urban irrigation*
- *the development of a 24-hour contact lens*
- *a greenhouse gas mitigation project involving the transport and deep geological storage of carbon dioxide.*

Innovations and discoveries

Government and private sector support, coupled with the talent of individual Australian scientists and researchers, has resulted in an impressive record of inventiveness and improved the lives of millions of people in many countries. Techniques and processes as commonplace as industrial refrigeration, the ready-mix system of transporting concrete and the use of polymer rather than paper for printing money were developed in Australia.

Other Australian inventions include the Synroc system for storing radioactive waste, the interscan microwave aircraft landing system, the black box flight data recorder, and smart proton probes for conducting research into materials and living cells.

Australia is also a great innovator in mining technology services. Australian companies have developed about 60 per cent of the world's mining software. They also lead in exploration assessment and mineral processing technologies, development of mining equipment, and scientific analysis technologies.

Australian scientists have also been responsible for many medical breakthroughs, including ultrasound scanners; the cochlear implant, designed to help the hearing impaired and the profoundly deaf; Relenza, the world's first anti-influenza drug, which was developed in 1996 and is now sold in more than 50 countries; and the SolarScan, developed in 1998, which can quickly detect cancerous moles.

Recent successes include:

- ground-breaking research on gastritis and peptic ulcers, for which two Australians, Professor Barry Marshall and Dr Robin Warren, were awarded the Nobel Prize in Physiology or Medicine in 2005
- the development in 2005 of a vaccine to prevent and treat cervical cancer by Professor Ian Frazer, a clinical immunologist.

Research leads to innovation and discovery.

REVISION EXERCISES 1.4

1. Define the term "performance objective".

   _____

   _____

   _____

2. Define e-commerce and explain how it works.

   _____

   _____

   _____

3. List and explain the **five** ways of ensuring that quality work is produced in a business.

   _____

   _____

   _____

   _____

   _____

4. Explain how the following operations strategies can improve business performance and output:

   a. Speed

   _____

   _____

   b. Dependability

   _____

   _____

   c. Flexibility

   _____

   _____

   d. Customisation

   _____

   _____

REVISION EXERCISES 1.4   **Page 2**

5. With new product or service design and development to make production more efficient, certain things need to be looked at. List and explain the seven things that business has to look at to ensure efficiency of production.

_____

_____

_____

_____

6. List and explain the other things that need to be considered.

_____

_____

_____

_____

7. Define e-commerce and explain how it works.

_____

_____

_____

_____

_____

8. Outline how globalisation has led to "global sourcing" and "vertical integration".

_____

_____

_____

_____

_____

_____

_____

_____

REVISION EXERCISES 1.4 **Page 3**

9. Explain the meaning of "outsourcing" and outline the advantages and disadvantages of this practice.

   _____

   _____

   _____

   _____

   _____

   _____

10. Outline how technology has been able to develop and promote production. In your answer include information on each of the types of technological developments of recent years.

    _____

    _____

    _____

    _____

    _____

    _____

11. Outline how technology has been able to develop and promote production. In your answer include information on each of the types of technological developments of recent years.

    _____

    _____

    _____

    _____

    _____

    _____

    _____

    _____

    _____

REVISION EXERCISES 1.4   **Page 4**

12. Inventory management is very important to the operations process.
Explain the importance of barcoding.

_____

_____

_____

_____

_____

_____

_____

_____

13. What do LIFO and FIFO stand for and explain how they
operate in a business?

_____

_____

_____

_____

_____

_____

_____

_____

14. Explain the Just-in-Time stock handling system.

_____

_____

_____

_____

_____

_____

_____

REVISION EXERCISES 1.4 **Page 5**

15. Explain the quality management systems of control, assurance and improvement.

_____

_____

_____

_____

_____

_____

_____

_____

_____

_____

_____

_____

_____

16. Outline the main reasons why some business managers resist change.

_____

_____

_____

_____

_____

_____

_____

_____

_____

_____

_____

_____

_____

_____

_____

_____

_____

_____

REVISION EXERCISES 1.4   **Page 6**

17. Describe the meaning of global sourcing and give some common examples.

_____

_____

_____

_____

_____

_____

18. Complete the table below relating to the advantages and disadvantages of global sourcing.

Advantages	Disadvantages

19. Describe the concept of scanning and learning.

_____

_____

_____

_____

_____

20. Why must businesses undertake "research and development"?

_____

_____

_____

_____

_____

_____

PRACTISE SHORT ANSWER STYLE QUESTIONS

(N.B. These are simulation questions only and may not necessarily be similar to actual HSC short answer questions. Marks allocated are guides only)

1. Mike has just started an educational retail book selling and printing business in Sydney's west. He is hoping to make the business as efficient as possible in terms of its operations and make it different to other similar businesses. He has asked you a series of questions.

   a. Define operations management. (2 marks)

   _____

   _____

   _____

   _____

   _____

   b. Explain the concept of cost leadership and describe **two** cost leadership strategies. (6 marks)

   _____

   _____

   _____

   _____

   _____

   c. Suggest **two** ways that Mike could differentiate his goods and services from other similar businesses. (2 marks)

   _____

   _____

   _____

   _____

   _____

2. Describe the influences that globalisation and technology have had on the operations process. (4 marks)

_____

_____

_____

_____

_____

3. Select **one** of the following and describe the effect that it could have on the production process: (6 marks)
   4. government policies
   5. legal regulations
   6. environmental sustainability

_____

_____

_____

_____

_____

7. Describe and analyse the difference between legal compliance and social responsibility in business. (5 marks)

_____

_____

_____

_____

_____

8. Describe and analyse the difference between environmental sustainability and social responsibility in business. (5 marks)

_____

_____

_____

_____

_____

9. As a builder Peter has to make sure that he completes jobs on time and make sure that he gets the scheduling of each task in order. In order to do this he uses a Gantt chart and a critical path analysis tool.
   Explain what Gantt charts and critical path analysis are.   (4 marks)

   _____

   _____

   _____

   _____

   _____

10. Explain how those tools can help with monitoring, controlling and improving his operations process.   (6 marks)

   _____

   _____

   _____

   _____

   _____

11. Most businesses have performance objectives designed as targets they want to reach. Select **five** of the following objectives and describe how they can help to improve the operations of a business: (10 marks)
    12. Quality
    13. Speed
    14. Dependability
    15. Flexibility
    16. Customisation
    17. Cost

   _____

   _____

   _____

   _____

   _____

   _____

   _____

   _____

   _____

   _____

   _____

   _____

   _____

18. When a business decides to go global and export some of its products, it has to consider the following:
   19. Logistics
   20. e-commerce
   21. Global sourcing

   a. Describe and account for the relevance of each of the above items in terms of business in the 21st century.   **(8 marks)**

_____

_____

_____

_____

_____

   b. Define outsourcing.   **(1 mark)**

_____

_____

_____

_____

_____

   c. Describe the difference between leading edge technology and established technology.   **(1 mark)**

_____

_____

_____

_____

_____

22. Philip was having problems with stock control in his warehouse until someone told him about LIFO, FIFO and JIT stock management systems

   a. Explain what each of these are.   **(6 marks)**

_____

_____

_____

   b. Account for the importance of each system to Philip.   **(4 marks)**

_____

_____

_____

13. Quality management is important to the operations of a business.

    a. Define quality management   (2 marks)

_____

_____

_____

    b. What is a management control system?   (2 marks)

_____

_____

_____

    c. Define quality assurance   (2 marks)

_____

_____

_____

    d. What is meant by continuous improvement?   (2 marks)

_____

_____

_____

14. Bronwyn and Elizabeth have decided to purchase some new and expensive computerised machinery in order to improve the operations of their business. They notice that some of their other partners and some staff are resisting the change to their working environment that this purchase will bring.

    a. Outline **two** possible reasons for this resistance
       to the change.   (2 marks)

_____

_____

_____

    b. Describe and analyse **two** global factors that may have influenced Bronwyn and Elizabeth's decision.   (6 marks)

_____

_____

_____

_____

_____

Glossary

Australian Securities and Investment Commission (ASIC): A government body established to monitor and regulate Australia's corporations, markets and financial services.

Australian Securities Exchange (ASX): The Australian Securities Exchange (ASX) provides a forum for businesses and individuals to buy and sell shares.

Awards: An award is an enforceable document containing minimum terms and conditions of employment in addition to any legislated minimum terms.

Balance Sheet: This statement gives a summary of the financial position of a business at a particular point in time. It shows the assets and liabilities of the business together with the value of owners equity in the business.

Banks: Secure organisation which uses funds deposited for investment by customers to provide cash and loans as required. Banks also exchange currencies and and provide a venue for financial transactions. As a group, banks are by far the largest financial providers in Australia.

Benchmarking refers to the establishment points of reference from which quality or excellence is measured.

Bills of exchange: (see commercial bills)

Budgets: Budgets are quantitative forecasts that help guide the use of the financial inputs and outgoings of a business.

Capital expenditure budget: A schedule setting out the planned expenditure on new machinery, buldings, plant and equipment.

Cash flow budget: A schedule of expected receipts and expenditure for a business. It differs from a cash flow statement, because it relates to future cash flows.

Cash flow statement: A cash flow statement is a summary of the movements of cash during a given period of time.

Certified Agreement: A certified agreement is an agreement made between employers and employees regarding wages and conditions in a workplace which has been ratified and approved by an appropriate tribunal or commission.

Commercial bills: These are known as bills of exchange. They are a form of short term (business) loan where a borrower agrees to repay a cash advance in 30 ,60 or 90 days as agreed.

Communication skills: Skills which enable people to understand each other. If a manager communicates effectively his plans will be followed and the business will grow.

Competitive positioning: Is about defining how you'll "differentiate" your offering and create value for your market.

Competitive pricing: This occurs when prices are set in relation to competitors prices.

Computer aided design (CAD): Design functions are automated by using computers.

Computer aided manufacture (CAM): This is software which allows the manufacturing process to become controlled by a computer.

Consumer markets: These consist of all the individuals and households who buy goods and services for personal consumption.

Contract manufacturing: The practice of outsourcing production instead of producing the function in house.

Contract worker: A contract worker hires his labour on an hourly basis, instead of becoming an employee.

Control: This is one of the managerial functions like planning, organizing, staffing and directing. In quality management, it is the operative stage, and may be used to describe all of these functions.

Corporate responsibility: The responsibility that business has to other businesses and the community generally.

Cost centre: A cost centre is a location, function or items of equipment monitored to determine operating costs for control purposes.

Cost control: Cost control involves careful purchasing, minimizing waste and efficient inventory control.

Cost leadership: This is an operating policy producing goods or services at the lowest cost possible to the business. Lower costs maximises profits, enabling business to establish a competitive advantage over its competitors.

Cost pricing: Selling goods at the producer's historical cost, i.e without making a profit.

Credit terms: These are the conditions of sale setting out how goods will be paid for, and the time to pay (30, 60 or 90 days).

Current assets: Consist of assets that can be turned into cash in a short period of time (usually within the accounting period). Current assets include cash, accounts receivable, inventories (which can be turned to cash quickly) and cash paid in advance.

Current liabilities: These are liabilities that may be called on in the short term (within one accounting period) and include accounts payable and overdrafts.

Customer orientation: When identifying consumer needs the marketer must identify what the consumer wants.

Customisation: Is the personalisation of products and services for individual customers.

Customise: To customise is to modify something according to a customer's individual requirements.

Data Miners: These are organisations which use huge data bases to pin point consumer preferences.

Debentures: A debenture is a loan to a company that is not necessarily secured by a mortgage on specific property but secured by the overall assets of the company.

Deceptive and misleading advertising: This occurs when, in the promotion of a product or service, a representation is made to the public that is false or misleading.

Demographics: Age, income, gender, marital status, sex, income etc

Derivatives: These are simple financial contracts whose value is linked to or derived from an underlying asset, such as stocks, bonds, commodities, loans and exchange rates.

De-skilling: This occurs when changed procedures (usually as a result of technology) removes a job that once required skill and replaces it with a job that doesn't.

Discounts: These are given on goods and services to encourage consumers to buy the product.

Discounts for early payments: Many businesses offer discounts to debtors for early payments as a means of improving cash flow.

Distribution channels: This covers the way in which a product is distributed from the factory to the consumer.

Double Loop learning: results in radical changes in the way the company does business. Double-loop learning allows the organisation to break out of existing thought patterns and to create a new mindset.

Effective profitability management: Refers to the maximisation of revenue and the minimisation of costs.

Efficiency: Describes how well a business is being run i.e. how efficiently the business is using its resources such as labour, finance or equipment.

e-marketing or electronic marketing: refers to the application of marketing principles and techniques via electronic media and more specifically the Internet.

Employees: People who work for employers for a wage or salary.

Employer associations: advise employers of their rights and obligations with regard to their employees and provide representation at Industrial Relations Commission (IRC) hearings where necessary.

Employers or management: is the group of people who own and manage a business.

Employment Contract: An employment contract is an agreement between an employer and employee/s that defines the rights and conditions for work.

Enterprise Agreement: An enterprise agreement is an agreement between an employer and an employee or employee group which covers wages and terms and conditions of work.

Equal Employment Opportunity (EEO): An employment policy where employees and employers have the responsibility to work to their full capacity, to recognise the skills and talents of other staff members to respect cultural and social diversity among colleagues and customers, to refuse to co-operate in, or condone any behaviour that may harass a colleague. (www.lawlink.nsw.gov.au)

Equity: Refers to the capital and accumulated funds and reserves shown in the balance sheet that is the owners share of a business.

Equity finance: The money (capital) put into a business by its owners. This may consist of cash, shares purchased in the business or retained profits. (See retained profits)

Exchange rate: i.e. the value of one currency against another.

Expense budgets: A forecast of all the activities of a business and the associated expenses involved.

Expense minimisation: A policy or practice of producing goods or services at the lowest possible cost or expenditure.

External funds: are the funds used in a business that have been obtained from a source outside the business. This is usually in the form of debt finance.

Factoring: This is the selling of accounts receivable to a financier. This is regarded as an important source of finance because the business is receiving immediate funds to use as working capital.

FIFO(First -In-First Out): An asset-management and valuation method in which the assets produced or acquired first are sold, used or disposed of first. FIFO may be used by a individual or a corporation.

Fixed cost: A fixed cost is a cost to a business that has to be made regardless of the level of output.

Flat Management Structures: As a response to change, flatter management structures have become more common over the past ten years. Businesses adopt a flatter management structure to reduce the number of levels of management, giving greater responsibility to middle managers.

Flexible employees: work flexible hours according to need. The conditions here are similar to casual employees unless a permanent employment agreement is decided on.

Flexible work practices: These are patterns of work that allow employees to vary their work commitments around the pressures of other responsibilities. They can assist employees in effectively managing work and family duties.

Foreign exchange (forex) market: The forex market is where currencies are traded by financial institutions acting as buyers and sellers.

Gantt chart: is a sequencing tool presented as a bar graph with time and activities shown on the two axes.

Global branding: This refers to the use of a brand name that is known world-wide.

Globalisation: Globalisation is the bringing together all of the world's economies for the purposes of trade and culture. It is the removing of barriers--trade barriers, language barriers, cultural barriers. It leads to the freeing up of the movement of labour from one country to another, the unification of laws and the unification of currency. It also involves financial flows, investment, technology and general economic behaviour in and between nations.

Global pricing: This is a contract between a customer and a supplier where the supplier agrees to charge the customer the same price for the delivery of parts or services anywhere in the world.

Global sourcing: This refers to the action of a business sourcing its raw materials from anywhere in the world. It is also a term used to describe the practice of sourcing raw materials from the global market for goods and services across geopolitical boundaries.

Goodwill: Goodwill is an intangible asset equal to that part of total assets which cannot be attributed to the separate business assets. In some ways it represents the synergy of the business.

Greenfields agreements: These involve a genuinely new enterprise that one or more employers are establishing or propose to establish and who have not yet employed persons necessary for the normal conduct of the enterprise. Such agreements may be either a single-enterprise agreement or a multi-enterprise agreement.

Growth: Business growth occurs with increased sales, by merging with other businesses or acquiring other businesses. In the balance sheet, growth is measured by the growth in the value of the business assets.

Head hunting: Recruitment by directly targeting a key individual who has the qualifications and characteristics that the firm is seeking. The prospect may already hold down a job in another business. The 'head hunter' usually makes an offer which, if accepted, enables the appointment to be made.

Historic cost: is the practice of valuing assets at the time of purchase.

Human Resource Management: This involves the use of qualified management staff in achieving the goals of the business, by ensuring that staff are productive, well-trained and satisfied in their jobs.

Implied conditions:

Consumers can expect the following when goods are sold:

1. the vendor is entitled to sell
2. the goods are unencumbered
3. the consumer has the right to quiet enjoyment
4. goods will comply with their description
5. goods will be of merchantable quality and fit for the purpose
6. goods will comply with a sample
7. services will be rendered with due care and skill
8. goods supplied with the service will be fit for purpose
9. services will be fit for the purpose.

Income statement: (see revenue/profit & loss statement)

Induction: This is the systematic introduction of new employees to their jobs, co-workers and the organisation. It may include on the job training.

Industrial markets: These are markets for goods and services which are used in the production of other goods and services and which are on sold to others in the production process.

Innovation: Innovation refers to the introduction of new systems, new technologies, approaches and products.

Inputs: These are the resources used in the process of production.

Intangibles: These are things such as patents, copyrights, trademarks and brand names and are often difficult to quantify.

Interest rates: are the price expressed as a percentage per annum for borrowing or lending money.

Intermediate goods: Those goods manufuctered from raw materials and then used to make a finished product.

Intermediate markets: Often known as reseller markets. These markets consist of businesses that acquire goods for the purpose of reselling them to others in order to make a profit.

Internal sources of finance: are those funds provided to the business by its owners and are in the form of retained profits.

Interpersonal skills: Effective managers are be able to interact with their staff to enable the business to run smoothly. Skilful communication ensures tasks are perfomed efficiently and productively

Inventories: Inventories are raw materials, goods in transit and complete and incomplete work (work in progress). Inventories are expensive and can often comprise 50% of working capital

Job design: Job design determines the way work is organised and performed. The process identifies the work to be done, how the job will be done, the skills, knowledge and abilities (capabilities) needed to do the job and how the job contributes to achieving organisational goals.

Kaizen: This is the Japanese concept of constantly seeking improvement and questioning current methods of production.

Leadership style: The manner and approach of providing direction, implementing plans, and motivating people.

Leasing: This is an agreement whereby the owner of an asset (lessor) allows the use of an asset by a lessee for a periodic charge.

LIFO (last-in-first-out): An asset-management and valuation method that assumes that assets produced or acquired last are the ones that are used, sold or disposed of first.

Line management: Management of a business concerned with acquiring, producing and supplying goods and services to consumers. (Other management is involved in supporting line managers pursue these objectives. Human resource and administration managers would fall into this support function.)

Liquidity: is the ability of a business to pay its short term obligations as they fall due.

List pricing: This is the price a product is set at on a sellers' schedule. The list price is the normal selling price without discounts.

Logistics: Logistics is the internal and external transport,storage and distribution resources of a business

Long-term borrowing: These are regarded as borrowings that will take longer than a year to repay.

Loss leader: A loss leader is a product sold at a low price (at cost or below cost) to stimulate other profitable sales.

Maintenance of human resources: This is the "keeping" of human resources by providing them with benefits such as a safe working environment, good pay and a fair and equitable industrial setting in which to work.

Management: Management is the process of integrating all the available resources of the business to achieve the aims of the organisation.

Management Consultant: A management consultant is someone from outside the business who, for a fee will come in to advise the business about problems with systems and procedures that the business cannot solve on its own.

Management control system: This is a system which gathers and uses information to evaluate the performance of different parts of the business or resources

Marketing: The coordination of activities that determine the product, price promotion and place (the Four P's) for a product or service.

Marketing aim: To meet the objectives of a business by satisfying a customer's needs and wants

Market penetration: This is strength of sales and marketing of the business and its product compared to the total market size.

Market pricing: This occurs where a business prices their product according to what the business feels the market can pay.

Marketing concept: The marketing plan or strategy adopted by a business seeking to satisfy consumer demand.

Market research: Is the systematic collection and analysis of information and findings relating to a marketing situation faced by a company.

Market Share: Expressed as a percentage of the available market for the product. For example if the total market is 100%, the share held by company X might be 6.5%

Market share analysis: This analysis involves comparing the market share of the business with ones competition.

Mentoring: This is a situation where a more experienced (usually older) staff member is assigned to look after the progress of a new employee in the workplace.

Middle Management: The level of management between top management and other workers. There may be a number of levels in a large business. Middle levels are progressively being reduced as business seeks greater efficiency and empathy with its staff.

Minimum employment standards: These relate to the minimum conditions under which an employee can be employed.

Mortgage: This is a loan giving a bank first claim over specified assets such as land or buildings which are used as security.

Motivation: This refers to the energy, direction, purpose and effort displayed by people in their activities.

Multi-enterprise agreements: These involve two or more employers that are not all single interest employers. competitors.

New issues (shares): This occurs when a private or public company wishes to raise more capital and issues a new issue of shares.

Niche markets: are small, specialised markets catering for a small clientele.

Nominal exchange rate risks: This refers to the risk of losing money on international transactions as a result of changes in the exchange rate i.e. a depreciation of the Australian dollar or an appreciation of the currency of the country we are dealing with thus forcing us to take a loss on the transaction.

Non-current assets: These are those assets that are held for a long period of time (longer than the accounting period). Assets that cannot easily be converted into cash.

Non-current liabilities: These are held for a long period of time (usually several years) and include mortgages and long-term borrowings.

Observation: This is the gathering of data through the observation of people, activity or results.

Operations/management: Operations or operations management can be described as the allocation and maintenance of machinery and resources (for example raw materials and labour), productivity, quality, wastage and the introduction of new technologies that will combine to produce a good or service. Operations may also refer to a wider sphere of production such as assembly, batching, creative design and packaging. It is sometimes also referred to as production management.

Outsourcing: This is a situation whereby a business contracts certain work "out" to professionals such as lawyers and accountants.

Operational planning: Making decisions about which groups or departments will be responsible for carrying out the various elements of the strategic plan, deciding what needs to be done, when, by whom and at what cost.

Opinion leaders: are used to promote a product by promoting it in written form or verbally.

Ordinary shares: These are shares issued to investors in companies that entitle purchasers (holders) to a part ownership of the business.

Outsourcing: This is a situation whereby a business contracts certain work "out" to professionals such as lawyers and accountants.

Overdrafts: An overdraft is an agreement between a bank and a business allowing the business to overdraw on its cheque account up to a certain, agreed figure.

Owners equity: This consists of funds placed into the business by its owners. They can also be described as the assets that the business holds on behalf of the owners and includes shares and retained profits.

Part-time employees: Can be permanent except they work reduced hours. For example a part-time teacher may work two or three days a week.

Payment period: These periods vary according to the amount borrowed and for what purpose. Borrowings may be free of interest for short periods or attract interest for longer periods.

Penetration pricing: This involves charging a very low price initially to generate high volume sales and gain market share. It is used to establish customers that will be loyal to the product in the long term.

People Skills: Those skills associated with the management of employees through leadership, good communication and interest in employees ambitions and progress.

Performance management: or appraisal is the process of assessing the performance of employees against actual results and expectations of the manager.

Permanent employees: Employees who hold down a job with security of tenure. They receive benefits such as compulsory superannuation, holiday pay and sick leave.

Physical evidence: Is the material part of a service. In marketing it may be the tickets, brochures or advertising: the non-physical part may be the entertainment of the spectacle provided by the sport.

Place: The methods of distribution, storage and delivery that are used for the product.

Political and default risk: This risk is associated with countries which have unstable governments or those that have a difficult balance of payments situation.

Potential market: is the set of consumers who have some level of interest in a product.

Price: The cost of the product in the market place together with the methods of pricing used, discounts or credit terms used.

Price discrimination: This occurs when a seller charges different prices to different consumers for the same product.

Price points: These are points where the price of a product is at its optimum i.e. at the point where a retailer will sell most of their products for maximum profit.

Price skimming: This can be applied to a new product that is attractive and which has little or no competition. A high price can be charged initially, but can only be maintained over the short term because the high price will attract competitors into the market and the new competition will force the price downwards.

Primary research: This involves collecting raw data from scratch i.e. data that has not been published elsewhere.

Process layouts: These are configurations in which operations of a similar nature or function are grouped together.

Product: All the different goods and services that are offered to customers, the way they are packaged and the types of after sales service offered.

Product approach: The product approach revolves around the idea that if producers produced products and services, then consumers would want them.

Product differentiation: can be defined as the variation between a number of models of the same basic product e.g. a brand of washing machine with six available models.

Product positioning: This is a key aspect of the marketing mix. It's the image a product has in the mind of a consumer. Products can be positioned in the market according to price and quality, image, target market or its competition.

Profitability: This refers to the yield or profit a business receives in return for its productive effort.

Proliferation: When a product category contains many brands with minor differences.

Promotion: This is the technique of presenting a product or service to a customer in such a way that the customer will want to purchase that product or service.

Promotional pricing: This involves a temporary reduction in price on a number of products on offer designed to increase sales in the short term and give the retail outlet a boost.

Public relations: This is any form of letting the customer know that a product exists and can involve any of the promotional methods. Publicity may involve such things as testimonial letters, word of mouth information, spotters fees and sponsorships of special events and sporting teams.

Quality assurance: The QA manager's role is to count, measure and report on all aspects of operations to enable the line manager to direct and supervise. QA reports will highlight any deviation from planned or standard performance and suggest what corrective action needs to be taken.

Quality Circles: These comprise groups of skilled employees gathered together in a process that aims to better the quality of a product/service or procedure that will benefit a customer or the business by decreasing unnecessary costs.

Quality control: This can be defined as the management procedures that are put in place to check the suitability of raw materials, progress of production and product output to minimise reprocessing, seconds, wastage, costs, warranty claims and service problems.

Quality Expectations: see **Quality Assurance**

Quality management: This involves control, assurance and improvement. It is a continuously cyclical process calling on all the entrepreneurial flair, innovative skills, experience, people management skills, decision making skills, communication skills that a manager has.

Recruitment: This involves the ways in which employees are acquired for the firm.

Redundancy payments: When a worker is no longer needed in the business, he becomes redundant, and receives compensation for losing his job.

Relationship marketing: A marketing strategy relying on a personal relationship with customers.

Research and Development: refers to "creative work undertaken on a systematic basis in order to increase the stock of knowledge, including knowledge of man, culture and society, and the use of this stock of knowledge to devise new applications" (OECD).

Resignation: The voluntary action taken by an employee to leave an employer.

Resistance to change: The unwillingness of employees or managers to embrace new practices. The source of change may be new technology, new inventions, new ideas or new stakeholders.

Resource markets: Are those markets for commodities such as minerals, agricultural products, people looking for work (human resources) and financial resources.

Retained profits: These are the profits retained by the business and which have not been distributed to the owners/shareholders in the form of dividends.

Return on capital: This is the percentage of profit before or after tax compared to the value of capital (money) invested in the business.

Revenue controls: These are aimed at maximising revenues received by the business through its business and financial activities.

Revenue/Profit & Loss Statement: This statement provides a summary of the trading operations of a business for a given period of time (usually one month or a year).

Robotics: The use of robots or automation to streamline operations, often eliminating boring repetitive tasks.

Sale and lease back: A device used by business to sell assets and lease them back from the purchaser. This then frees up capital that can be used for other purposes.

Sales mix: This refers to the mix of the products produced and offered for sale by a business.

Sales objectives: These relate to the concept of increasing and maximising sales in order to maximise revenue.

Scanning and Learning: is a process of gathering, analysing, and dispensing business information for tactical (short term) or strategic (long term) purposes.

Scheduling: This involves the time taken to complete a particular job.

Secondary research: Data that is already in existence and usually collected by someone else for some other purpose.

Seconds: These are goods which have failed to meet the design or quality standards of the business.

Security: The charge given over an asset or assets which will be given over to a lender if the borrower defaults on a loan.

Short-term borrowing: This is made up of overdrafts and commercial bills and is normally used when the business requires finance for a relatively short time of up to a year or when the finance is required to assist with working capital.

Separation of human resources: This is the business term that describes the reduction of staff numbers for a variety of reasons, including retirement and redundancy (including voluntary and involuntary redundancy).

Sequencing: This involves placing tasks into an order so that an operation runs smoothly.

Sales promotion: Sales promotions may take several different forms. A trade fair such as a motor show, computer show, sports or leisure show is one form of sales promotion. The producer demonstrates his/her wares in an area set aside for that particular business while potential customers can walk by and observe the products on show.

Secondary Industry: The industrial sector of an economy dominated by the manufacture of finished products.

Secondary target market: This is the second most important market identified as a consumer group for the output of the business.

Self-managing: Employees in a self managed business work in an autonomous fashion without the need for constant supervision.

Situation analysis: A situation analysis is an assessment of a business's current position, e.g. its market share, profitability or competition

Stakeholders: Stakeholders are those people or institutions with an interest in a business in some way.

Strategic alliance: A strategic alliance occurs where two or more businesses work together to achieve a particular goal.

Strategic analysis: Strategic analysis is the examination of a business in the light of long term (3 to 5 years) goals and objectives. It will usually consider budgets, forecasts and prospects

Strategic planning: Strategic planning is long term planning (3 to 5 years).

Strategic thinking: This is the ability to think beyond the immediate tasks.

Target market: This is a section of the public to whom the producer aims his/her products and marketing campaigns.

Teamwork: The ability to work together. If the manager is a "team player" he will inspire teamwork in employees.

Training: This is the preparation of employees to undertake existing or new tasks proficiently.

Variable costs: Those costs only incurred when something is produced, such as direct labour or raw materials used. They vary directly with the volume of sales or production.

Vision: This is the ability of management to see where the business needs to go in the future and what is required to succeed. It is also the ability to see the "big picture" with regard to business direction.

Voluntary administration: This is a process under the Corporations Act. It allows a caretaker (the voluntary administrator) to take control of the affairs of a company while the directors are given a chance to propose a resolution of the company's financial problems to its creditors.

Voluntary separation and Involuntary separation: Voluntary separation occurs when an employee leaves of their own free will. Involuntary separation occurs when an employee loses their job as a result of an employer's action.